Joint Military Intelligence College

July 2003

I0429268

SHAKESPEARE FOR ANALYSTS: LITERATURE AND INTELLIGENCE

Occasional Paper Number Ten

The Joint Military Intelligence College supports and encourages research on intelligence issues that distills lessons and improves support to policy-level and operational consumers

This series of Occasional Papers presents the work of faculty, students and others whose research on intelligence issues is supported or otherwise encouraged by the Joint Military Intelligence College through its Center for Strategic Intelligence Research. Occasional Papers are distributed to Department of Defense schools and to the Intelligence Community, and unclassified papers are available to the public through the National Technical Information Service (www.ntis.gov). Selected papers are also available through the U.S. Government Printing Office (www.gpo.gov).

Proposed manuscripts for these papers are submitted for consideration to the Center for Strategic Intelligence Research Editorial Board. Papers undergo review by senior officials in Defense, Intelligence and occasionally civilian academic or business communities. The editor wishes to thank JMIC faculty member Col Tim Christenson (USMCR) and Mr. James McDevitt of the DIA Joint Military Intelligence Training Center for their invaluable comments on drafts of this paper. Manuscripts or requests for additional copies of Occasional Papers should be addressed to Defense Intelligence Agency, Joint Military Intelligence College, Center for Strategic Intelligence Research, MC-X, Bolling AFB, Washington, DC 20340-5100.

Russell.Swenson@dia.mil, Editor

Occasional Paper Number Ten

SHAKESPEARE FOR ANALYSTS: LITERATURE AND INTELLIGENCE

Jeffrey White

WASHINGTON, DC
July 2003

CONTENTS

FOREWORD

Will Washington, DC's Folger Theater realize a sharp increase in attendance by analysts of the U.S. Intelligence Community as a result of the appearance of this monograph? That is a distinct possibility. Jeff White, for nearly 35 years one of the Defense Intelligence Agency's most distinguished military analysts until his retirement in late 2002, would like to see that happen. And the reader of this monograph will quickly learn why. His argument is that a good understanding of Shakespeare's art can contribute to improved intelligence analysis.

For those who have worked and enjoyed life with the author, Jeff White is the consummate military intelligence analyst. His forté is military history, and over the years I found him articulate and skillful in assessing military campaigns—from Thermopyle to Agincourt to Waterloo to Gettysburg to Verdun to El Alamein to Abu Ageila to Val Fajr II. For a number of years, he taught a course at the then-Defense Intelligence College in which Middle East conflicts were examined through the lens of military campaigns. But of the nearly 25 years we worked together, I never learned of his abiding interest in Shakespeare—until that day in late 2002, shortly before his retirement, when the manuscript for this Occasional Paper appeared on my computer screen.

In addition to being an outstanding and influential analyst, Jeff was also during the last 20 years of his career a well-respected leader of analysts. I interpret the appearance of this manuscript at the twilight of his government intelligence career as yet another effort at exerting leadership. So you want to be a fine intelligence analyst, asks the former master of the trade? Here is a secret—Shakespeare!!!

At first I was skeptical, but from page one, as I began to perceive the author's "analysis," I started to see the point. In the scientifically-ordered approach to reality that has come to dominate modern Western man, including intelligence analysts, we often "get it wrong." White's appeal is for a revival of the humanities-based appreciation of knowledge as a factor in assessing, interpreting, and predicting human interactions. And where better to start than with the Master himself?

When you think about it—unfortunately I had to read this monograph before I thought about it—Shakespeare's interests coincided in many ways with the daily preoccupations of intelligence analysts: coups d'etat (Richard II), political assassination (Julius Caesar), civil wars and international wars (Henry V, Henry VI—Agincourt, War of the Roses), political tyranny (Richard III), political/military leadership (all of the above, but White focuses on Henry V). White considers them excellent analytical case studies. Although Shakespeare may have been an imperfect historian—the artist by definition creates a "distorted" reality—and his characters may be somewhat overdrawn, I believe White would say they inform us all the more because of their larger-than-life stature. This monograph was written before Operation IRAQI FREEDOM in March-April 2003, so the occasional references to Iraqi dictator Saddam Hussein may seem a bit dated. But now the reader may be in an even better position to evaluate White's claim that understanding Richard III, as Shakespeare presents him to us, helps us to enter the mind of a tyrant like Saddam Hussein.

I must let the reader decide whether the author's key argument has merit. I believe it does. But whatever the case, this work has value. It reawakened in me an interest in Shakespeare. It had not occurred to me to conceptualize Shakespeare from the perspective of the intelligence analyst. Shakespeare becomes fascinating from this perspective. I believe Shakespeare, as White argues, does help inform us regarding the key questions that intelligence analysts habitually ask. Why do some men covet power? What is it like to usurp power? What is it like to lose power? What are the limits on the exercise of power and the use of force? When does the decision to use force emerge? How does violence expand? What kinds of behavior and actions does use of violence produce? How is violence justified by both sides of a conflict? How do unintended consequences emerge from carefully planned events? All these and many more are explored by White in this finely written essay. The reader will learn a lot about Shakespeare by reading it. The reader will also think more deeply about intelligence analysis by a close study of this paper.

Intelligence analysis is often the "art" of credible prediction on the basis all-too-incomplete evidence. Understanding the essence of human nature, especially as it operates in cultures foreign to our own, plays a most important role in compensating for insufficient evidence. White reminds us that the tribal and religiously animated England of the 15th and 16th centuries was a society akin to many of the societies and countries that preoccupy intelligence analysts today. We can learn a lot from knowing about that era, and White's perspective is that Shakespeare is the best window we have into that age. One doesn't have to know Shakespeare to appreciate this essay, but I assure you it will draw a reader closer to Shakespeare and perhaps make him or her an improved intelligence analyst in the process. It would not be surprising if readers became regular devotees of the Folger Theater as a consequence.

Max L. Gross
Dean, School of Intelligence Studies
Washington, DC
June 2003

SHAKESPEARE FOR ANALYSTS:
LITERATURE AND INTELLIGENCE

Thus far, with rough and all-unable pen,
Our bending author hath pursued the story,
In little room confining mighty men,
Mangling by starts the full course of their glory.

Henry V

INTRODUCTION

This paper is an argument and a suggestion. The argument is that what Shakespeare had to say about human behavior in the political and leadership realms is worth reading, and hearing, today. The suggestion is that analysts concerned with understanding the behavior of important individuals—leaders, commanders, supporters, family members, enemies, rivals, inner circle members, opposition figures—should do so. It is perhaps an "out of the box" idea; but I would contend that Shakespeare should be part of the canon of intelligence literature, a fundamental addition to the works that intelligence professionals read.

More precisely, I see great literature as a potential source of expertise that can be applied to intelligence issues of current interest. I would argue that today's analysts are dominated by two camps of thought, in a fashion akin to the two cultures identified long ago by C.P. Snow—science and social science,[1] a focus that left little room for attention to the third culture with which he was most concerned: the humanities. Although we have people with humanities or literature degrees, we do not use much of what they have learned, except perhaps for their writing skills. At this time, we cannot speak of a humanities-based approach to analysis, as we can of functional (science) or regional (social science) approaches.

I think this shortcoming causes us to miss something. Intelligence problems, at least those not in the science arena, are so difficult that we need to consider and actively pursue all potential sources of insight. Study of the humanities, and especially of literature, can help. Reading and studying literature expands the imagination, and analysts need imagination to make inferences, to bridge gaps in information, to see patterns, in other words, for discovery. Those who study literature learn to interpret. This is the essence of "sense making." Literature can assist us in the area of "storytelling." Good literature has an affective dimension, which is conveyed to its students. Good storytelling engages and convinces in ways that traditional intelligence reporting and analysis do not. We do not want to write pure fiction, although I would suggest that there might be a place for a form of

---

[1] C. P. Snow, *The Two Cultures* (Cambridge: Cambridge University Press), 1998.

historical fiction in intelligence "storytelling"; but we do want what we write to be read, understood, and absorbed. We want, in Russ McDonald's words, "... to create a community of thought and feeling" between our consumers and us.[2] This is especially important as analysis, particularly functional analysis, becomes more and more specialized. *What does it all mean?* is a more important and difficult question than *What does this piece mean?* Good literature is overwhelmingly concerned with human behavior, and it is in understanding human behavior that we are likely to get the most help from the humanities. Literature provides many powerful character studies, images, models, and metaphors of people acting and thinking under a wide range of circumstances. These should be available to analysts to draw upon.

More directly even than that is the approach implicit in Shakespeare: the recognition and then exploration of the complexity and diversity of the human element as the mainspring for achieving understanding, even wisdom, regarding the reality of political behavior. Machiavelli, who addressed many of the same issues as Shakespeare, and like Shakespeare was an acute observer of political man, wrote about political behavior, as it *ought* to be.[3] He was prescribing. Shakespeare wrote about political behavior as it is. He was illuminating. According to Alexander Leggatt, Shakespeare's "interest is not in examining what political structures best serve the general good, but in watching how people behave within the structures they have."[4] We have many tools to assist analysts, but few if any allow us to explore the behavioral and cognitive worlds of political and military leaders and those around them as effectively as does Shakespeare.

This is not a suggestion for everyone. Shakespeare is difficult, but rewarding. He provides a mirror for reflecting on political and social behavior, a mirror, which, if held at the right angle, produces powerful models, metaphors, and images that illuminate.

THE CHALLENGE

The range of issues faced by intelligence analysts is enormous: from questions of the most intricate detail to the broadest problems of policy and forecasting. To these questions analysts bring a variety of tools, methods, and experiences. Through skillful application they are able to resolve, or at least reduce, some of the uncertainty surrounding the issues they face. Success is most readily found when the questions concern "things": order of battle, infrastructure, facilities, air defense sites, and the technical capabilities of weapons. These involve questions of fact, or what is within the physical world and discoverable much of the time through traditional intelligence tools and techniques.

---

[2] Russ McDonald, *Shakespeare and the Arts of Language* (Oxford: Oxford University Press), 2001. 10.

[3] Tim Spiekerman, *Shakespeare's Political Realism: The English History Plays* (New York: State University of New York Press, 2001), 26.

[4] Alexander Leggatt, *Shakespeare's Political Drama: the History Plays and the Roman Plays* (New York: Routledge, 1988), 238.

More difficult is determining how these "things" work as "systems." The analyst must come to understand how and for what purpose the components of a system work together, for what ends, and to what effect. Dynamic elements and processes become subjects of interest. Understanding "systems" of "things" can be a difficult challenge, but not the most difficult.

A third, and most difficult, set of problems involves the people that command, order, and employ the systems. These problems are in the realm of human behavior, and in this realm the analyst faces the complexities of cognition, social interaction, and adaptive behavior, with their associated and consequent uncertainty and unpredictability. Unfortunately, but also intriguingly, for intelligence professionals, many of the key questions they are asked fall into this realm. Questions such as: What is the future direction of the Iranian government?; How will Iran respond to the threat of regime change?; At what point, or will, a dictator like Saddam concede defeat?; What are Chinese intentions toward Taiwan?; How stable is Bashar Asad's Syrian regime?; and Who is aiming to succeed him? Traditional intelligence methods often can only partially answer these kinds of questions. Some additional assistance is provided by modern techniques borrowed from psychology and sociology; but the analyst is often left with only their own understanding of, or feeling for, how human "targets" think, how this thinking is linked to action, and for what purposes. When the issues are important and the stakes are high, "feeling" is not enough.

WHY READ SHAKESPEARE AS AN ANALYST?

In our day, when dead European white males are being expunged from the curriculum, why still read Shakespeare? He is unquestionably dead, European, white, and male. [5]

Reaching back 400 years to an "old dead Englishman" to find help in answering important questions of current intelligence interest seems a leap; but I would make three arguments to support the purposeful reading of Shakespeare: He is indeed relevant, he provides insight into human behavior, and he provides multifaceted perspectives on people in important roles and complex events. In Tim Spiekerman's words,[6] Shakespeare "...is a keen observer of political practice with an eye for the permanent political problems."

Shakespeare's relevance to modern analysts is based on the material he addressed in many of his plays. Shakespeare chose as core subject matter for his histories and some tragedies a number of the principal political and military events and figures of English and ancient history. His source material was the best scholarship of the time regarding the history of England and the ancient world. If imbued with a Tudor perspective, this history was mediated through Shakespeare's profound ability to represent the full range and complexity of human behavior.

---

[5] David Bevington, *Shakespeare* (Oxford: Blackwell Publishing, 2002), 1.
[6] Spiekerman, *Shakespeare's Political Realism*, 17.

Furthermore, he wrote in a period of intensely interesting political activity. Even as he wrote to entertain, he also wrote to inform a sophisticated audience familiar with the recent history of England, and intensely involved in its political life. Among the important political events and issues of the time were the Northern Rebellion of 1569, the Ridolphi plot of 1572, the Babington Plot of 1586, continuing concern with foreign invasion and internal uprising, a sustained struggle between Protestants and Catholics for control of the monarchy, and uncertainty over succession. Shakespeare's relevance was accepted in his time. Elizabeth I stated at one point "I am Richard II," and during her reign the deposition scene from the play was censored. [7]

As Sir Ian McKellen put it in an interview about his lead role in the 1995 film version of *Richard III*: "It isn't the story of the nation. It's the story of the people who control the nation."[8] These kings, queens, and other "magnates," their close associates ("affinities"), and their enemies and rivals all provided the human material for Shakespeare's works. His tragedies also focused on the behavior of important political and military figures (some historical and some legendary) and their associates from antiquity. By focusing on the central figures of key historical events, Shakespeare could observe people under conditions of significant stress, uncertainty, and opportunity—the same conditions faced by the powerful in his audience. Together, this human and historical material constituted a vast laboratory for examining human behavior. In the words of one authority: "Shakespeare watches, moment by moment, the way his political figures impress others, and themselves, the means they use to do so, and the price they pay." [9]

Shakespeare cut and trimmed from his sources, and did not always relate history accurately; but in the doing he gave us vivid recreations of the thought and behavioral worlds of some of the most powerful figures in English and ancient history. Arguably these portraits bring us closer to the reality of these characters than standard historical works. As Tim Spiekerman wrote of *King John:*

> As is typical of his English history plays, the plot of Shakespeare's *King John* is driven by a violent struggle for political power. It features conspiracy, treason, assassination, moral corruption, poisoning, civil war, and foreign conquest.[10]

Much of Shakespeare's body of work addresses human behavior in contexts of enduring intelligence interest: inner-circle behavior; political relationships; the effects of asymmetries in culture, power, and personality; international war; coalition warfare; civil war; hierarchy; legitimacy; succession; rivalry and faction; loyalty; political violence; the analysis of motives; and the handling of ambiguity and uncertainty. Through Shakespeare we can gain sophisticated perspectives on the personalities and behaviors of modern leaders and the events they are involved in. Shakespeare made the most of his material, and we can too.

---

[7] Spiekerman, *Shakespeare's Political Realism,* 72.
[8] Interview with Sir Ian McKellen, *http://www.r3.org/onstage/FILM/mckella.html.*
[9] Leggatt, *Shakespeare's Political Drama,* xi.
[10] Spiekerman, *Shakespeare's Political Realism,* 39.

WHY NOT READ SHAKESPEARE?

One criticism of drawing on Shakespeare the way I am suggesting is that he and the material he used were products of the "Western" cultural experience, and therefore can only with difficulty, if at all, be applied to people and situations coming out of different cultures—Saddam Hussein was a 21st Century Arab leader, not a 15th Century English king or Roman politician. Adda Bozeman, for example has argued that culture is essential to the understanding of political life:

> ... the challenge of understanding "others"—be they friend or foes—can be met only after one has found out how they think. And since thought can be assumed to precede action in all human societies, I concluded that inquiry and analysis should focus on mental and moral persuasions be they religious, philosophical, or ideological; on basic values and norms within each society, and on time-transcendent perceptions of the other world. [11]

I believe there are several ways to respond to this. First, even though Arab and Western cultures are different, it is not necessarily true that individual Arabs will behave in fundamentally different ways than individual Englishmen when placed in similar situations. Shakespeare was dealing in many cases with basic human behavior rather than the norms of culture writ large. Indeed much of his work shows the failure of those norms to be controlling in the behavior of individuals. The medieval code of Chivalry and Roman Catholicism established widely accepted norms in the Middle Ages, very much along Bozeman's lines; but these were often "honored in the breach," as individuals acted according to their own motivation in the face of particular circumstances. [12]

Second, the widespread acceptance of Shakespeare's work across many cultures and times suggests that he was indeed addressing elemental human behavior. The personalities he created are found in many non-Western societies, not just Occidental or English. Both Jonathan Bate[13] and Harold Bloom[14] make the case that Shakespeare is not only read and performed in many cultures, but also that he is understood and interpreted across these cultures in terms of their own experience. As Bloom wrote of Shakespeare's work in *The Western Canon:*

> Clearly the phenomenon of surpassing literary excellence, of such power of thought, characterization and metaphor that it triumphantly survives translation and transportation and compels attention in virtually every culture, does exist.[15]

---

[11] Adda Bozeman, *Politics and Culture in International History: From the Ancient Near East to the Opening of the Modern Age,* 2d ed. (New Brunswick: Transaction Publishers, 2002), 5.

[12] Barbara Tuchman, *A Distant Mirror: The Calamitous 14th Century* (New York; Ballantine Books, 1978), xix.

[13] Jonathan Bate, *The Genius of Shakespeare* (London: Picador, 1998), 221-224.

[14] Harold Bloom, *The Western Canon: the Books and School of the Ages* (New York: Riverhead Books, 1994), 50.

[15] Bloom, *The Western Canon,* 49.

The *Oxford Companion to Shakespeare* lists the Arab World, China, East, West, and Southern Africa, India, Japan, and Korea among the non-Western regions or countries into which Shakespeare's works have been imported and interpreted. The Arab world has a number of Shakespearean scholars, playwrights, and actors.[16] In China, although his works did not appear until 1903, Shakespeare is widely appreciated, studied deeply, and is said to have attained the same prestige as Marx.[17] Shakespeare's introduction into India was through British rulers, but his works have now been widely adapted to Indian themes and culture.[18]

A second criticism might be that the events Shakespeare wrote about and his perspective on them were from an age so distant from ours that they are irrelevant to our time. But Shakespeare's unequalled understanding of human behavior, his ability to represent, even create,[19] the current of cognition that underlies human motivation and action, and, very importantly, his concern with the same kinds of issues, contexts, and behaviors that interest intelligence analysts and consumers today, make him relevant now. I think Barbara Tuchman had it right in her introduction to *A Distant Mirror:*

> People of the Middle Ages existed under mental, moral, and physical circumstances so different from our own as to constitute almost a foreign civilization. As a result, qualities of conduct that we recognize as familiar amid these alien surroundings are revealed as permanent in human nature.[20]

The opening quotation to this paper illustrates the difficulty Shakespeare recognized in the task; but none have represented human behavior better, especially the behavior of leaders and those they led. Shakespeare's characters appear as thinking, or cognitive, agents; it is his re-creation of thought and related action rather than his retelling of history that is important.

READING SHAKESPEARE

Reading Shakespeare requires an investment of time and concentration, and the application of interpretative and imaginative skills.[21] English as we know it was only being created, not least of all by Shakespeare himself, at the time he wrote, and grammar and word usage were much more flexible.[22] Additionally, Shakespeare was writing plays, not novels or history. What he wrote was intended for performance, and this has implications.

---

[16] Rafiq Darraji, "Arab World," in *The Oxford Companion to Shakespeare,* eds. Michael Dobson and Stanley Wells (Oxford: Oxford University Press, 2001), 20.

[17] Quixin He, "China," in *The Oxford Companion to Shakespeare,* eds. Michael Dobson and Stanley Wells (Oxford: Oxford University Press, 2001, 76.

[18] Ania Loomba, "India," in *The Oxford Companion to Shakespeare,* eds. Michael Dobson and Stanley Wells (Oxford: Oxford University Press, 2001), 212-213.

[19] Harold Bloom, *Shakespeare: the Invention of the Human* (New York: Riverhead Books, 1998), xviii

[20] Tuchman, xiv.

[21] John Russell Brown, *Shakespeare and the Theatrical Event* (New York: Palgrave MacMillan, 2002), 36; Leggatt, *Shakespeare's Political Drama,* 242.

[22] McDonald, 10.

One is that writing for the theater permits reduction and simplification for the sake of clarification and dramatization.[23] A single action or piece of dialogue can stand for a much more complicated or extended process or action. Also in Shakespeare's plays time and action are often compressed or reordered in order to heighten dramatic effect or make the author's point. Events that took years in historical time can follow one another rapidly in the plays. This can be disconcerting to those used to history delivered chronologically, but it can also heighten dramatic effect and give emphasis to related events or actions.

A third implication is that the plays demand active interpretation by the reader or audience member.[24] Reflecting the complexity and ambiguity of human behavior, Shakespeare does not wrap everything up for us neatly. Neither his characters nor his audiences have all the answers. Just as with the real analytical issues we face today, questions of motivation, intention, personality, behavior, and consequences are subject to differing interpretation and can remain unresolved.

The text segments used in this paper are taken from Internet versions of Shakespeare's works. There are two Internet sites from which I have drawn texts: "The Works of the Bard" at *http://www.it.usyd.edu.au/~matty/Shakespeare* and "Electronic Shakespeare: Resources for Researchers" at *http://www.wfu.edu/~tedforrl/shakespeare*. I have used segments of text from the plays to make the desired points. Although pulling them out of context has some associated risk ("Now is the winter of our discontent" refers to good times), quoting directly and on occasion at length serves several purposes. It illustrates precisely how Shakespeare framed the situations and recreated the events and behavioral worlds he was interested in. It permits the reader who is interested in deeper understanding to become increasingly experienced with 16th century English verse and prose. Very importantly, it provides a window into a different culture, and it is useful for analysts to gain experience looking through such windows. Many of the passages will require more than one reading for clear appreciation. I strongly recommend use of an annotated text of the plays. The *Arden, New Cambridge, or Folger* texts are excellent. Where citing text I have chosen to simply use the play title, act number, and scene number (e.g. *Richard II*, Act 5, Scene 1) as employed in the Internet versions. Where referring to a history play that has several parts, as with *Henry VI*, I have used the convention of citing the "part" first, as in *3 Henry VI* meaning *Henry VI, Part 3*. Where necessary for clarity I have made annotations in brackets within the text.

As might be expected there is a wealth of material on Shakespeare and politics. Innumerable courses are taught on this subject at the undergraduate and graduate levels. There is a significant body of commentary dealing with Shakespeare's personal politics and his view of the political world. I found Alexander Leggatt's *Shakespeare's Political Drama: The History Plays and the Roman Plays*, and Tim Spiekerman's *Shakespeare's Political Realism: The English History Plays*, especially useful. Three excellent works placing the history plays in context are *Shakespeare's Kings*, by John Julius Norwich; *Shakespeare's*

---

[23] Leggatt, Shakespeare's *Political Drama*, 242.
[24] Leggatt, Shakespeare's *Political Drama*, 242.

English Kings by Peter Saccio; and *William Shakespeare, the Wars of the Roses, and the Historians* by Keith Dockray. For a conventional history of the Wars of the Roses see John Gillingham's *The Wars of the Roses: Peace and Conflict in Fifteenth-Century England.*

APPROACH, FORMAT, AND SELECTION OF ISSUES

My approach to the subject matter was to first decide, based on my own experience, what I thought were high-interest issues for intelligence analysts. Once these were decided, I then developed a set of questions to guide the examination of the play or plays that seemed to have the most relevance to the basic issue. Not all of these questions are addressed in the discussions of the plays, and some other questions arose as I went along; but I have included them at the beginning of each relevant section to indicate how an intelligence analyst might approach a purposeful reading of a Shakespearean text. The main body of each section contains the discussion of the play or plays related to the issue under consideration.

Shakespeare's material is so rich in political and other human behavior that it was necessary to be selective.[25] The themes I have chosen include: What are the essential qualities of successful political leaders and military commanders? Why do some leaders—even those with talent—fail? What do the pure pursuit of power and the exercise of unbridled force look like? What are the human dynamics of a civil war? What is it like to be inside a coup as it unfolds? Why are family affairs politically important? What are the political roles of women—even in traditional societies? What is the political landscape of loyalty? These questions seem to be of enduring interest to political and leadership analysts, and Shakespeare explored them all.

Importantly, this paper is an interpretation—my interpretation—of the political and cognitive content of some of Shakespeare's plays. Other observers can interpret differently, see other elements, and stress other topics. A great deal depends on what one brings to the reading. But there is a potential common starting point: the recognition that there is significant political and human behavioral content in Shakespeare.

HEROIC LEADERSHIP: HENRY V

England ne'er had a king until his time.
Virtue he had, deserving to command:
What should I say? his deeds exceed all speech:
He ne'er lift up his hand but conquered.

1 Henry VI, Act 1, Scene 1

In considering Henry V as a representation of heroic leadership there were a number of questions that seemed relevant to intelligence analysts. How did he prepare for his future role? How did he exercise leadership? Was he self-aware in doing this? How did others—

---

[25] See for example, Spiekerman, *Shakespeare's Political Realism,* 14

allies, enemies, and subordinates—see him? What was his response to the possibility of failure and defeat? How did he manage the uncertainty he faced? How did he weigh the responsibility that he had to carry? These questions seem relevant to any leader in a non-trivial position of power.

How does in fact an analyst evaluate a foreign leader? How can he or she distill the essential qualities of distant individuals, determine from the dry text of messages and reports, or a few snatches of video tape, what manner of person they are looking at? In *Henry V*, Shakespeare presents us with a piece of high-quality leadership analysis, re-creating in a way a purely historical text cannot an awesomely dominating character. Shakespeare is able to illuminate for us a remarkably effective military commander and political strategist capable of winning against odds and exploiting military success with shrewd diplomacy. Henry V is a soldier-statesman in modern terms. Not many modern leaders have to combine military and political skills as Henry V did, but some do, including many "warlords" of intelligence interest. Henry is in a sense a benchmark "warlord" against which to measure the current and future "crops." But, through Shakespeare, we are able to more than just read about him; we are able to enter a recreation of his thought world.

From the very first lines in the play, which is built around war with France, we are made to understand that Henry is not someone who would be welcome in the councils of the European Union:

Chorus
>Then should the warlike Harry [Henry V], like himself,
>Assume the port of Mars; and at his heels,
>Leash'd in like hounds, should famine, sword and fire
>Crouch for employment.

>*Henry V,* Prologue

The first point Shakespeare makes about Henry V is that he has been a surprise. His wild youth, detailed in 1 and 2 *Henry IV,* proves to have been an effective training ground for a king, against all expectations based on performance. A bishop discusses Henry V's transformation:

Canterbury
>The courses of his youth promised it not.
>The breath no sooner left his father's body,
>But that his wildness, mortified in him,
>Seem'd to die too; yea, at that very moment
>Consideration, like an angel, came

>*Henry V,* Act 1, Scene 1

As becomes clear, much of this wildness was young Harry's conscious but unseen preparation for a leadership role, through close study of his subjects and the art of ruling.

Henry V's unanticipated emergence as a leader of quality serves as a warning to be cautious when assessing new leaders, especially when there is only limited information about past performance to go on. Henry himself warns the Dauphin, the heir to the French throne, that he has underestimated the English King:

> And we [Henry] understand him [the French Dauphin] well,
> How he comes o'er us with our wilder days,
> Not measuring what use we made of them.
> *Henry V,* Act 1, Scene 2

The Dauphin is unimpressed and during a French council of war makes his case:

> For, my good liege, she [England] is so idly king'd,
> Her scepter so fantastically borne
> By a vain, giddy, shallow, humorous youth,
> That fear attends her not.
> *Henry V,* Act 2, Scene 4

Not all the French think lightly of Harry, and the French King, recalling recent military defeats at the hands of the English, responds with a much different estimate than his son:

King of France
> Think we King Harry strong;
> And, princes, look you strongly arm to meet him.
> The kindred of him hath been flesh'd upon us;
> And he is bred out of that bloody strain
> That haunted us in our familiar paths:
> *Henry V,* Act 2, Scene 4

The second aspect of Henry that we are made aware of is that he is a calculating decisionmaker. In the second scene we see him weighing carefully a proposed invasion of France. He wants justification for the invasion; he wants to know if it will advance England's interests, and he wants to know whether the risks are manageable. He gathers and uses information and opinion from his advisors as he makes his decision:

King Henry V
> Now are we well resolved; and, by God's help,
> And yours, the noble sinews of our power,
> France being ours, we'll bend it to our awe,
> Or break it all to pieces:
> *Henry V,* Act 1, Scene 2

Henry takes action based on good intelligence on the situation in France, and his understanding of the political divisions that weaken the French.

Henry also knows how to act like a king. Tim Spiekerman in his analysis of *Henry V* devotes considerable attention to Henry's calculated role playing,[26] and Alexander Leggatt also sees Henry as playing various roles: "Responsible statesman, bloody conqueror, good fellow—Henry plays them all..."[27] His presence is commanding as he dominates almost any situation, or scene, he is in. His meeting with the French ambassador in the first act demonstrates his potent charisma as he turns the Dauphin's insult back on him and France:

Tell you the Dauphin I am coming on,
To venge me as I may and to put forth
My rightful hand in a well-hallow'd cause.
So get you hence in peace; and tell the Dauphin
His jest will savour but of shallow wit,
When thousands weep more than did laugh at it.
            Henry V, Act 1, Scene 2

In performance, Henry's dominance of the scene and the French ambassador is even clearer. In scenes such as the siege of Harfleur, Henry commands the attention of his men and the audience:

King Henry V
I see you stand like greyhounds in the slips,
Straining upon the start. The game's afoot:
Follow your spirit, and upon this charge
Cry "God for Harry, England, and Saint George!"
            Henry V, Act 3, Scene 2

And of course they do.

Henry's ability to draw the appropriate response from his men is a determining factor in his success. He is capable of winning and keeping their loyalty under even the most difficult circumstances. And he is capable of winning others to his cause and to make them believe in it, not just accept it. In Tim Spiekerman's words: "Simply put, Henry makes men proud to be alive under his rule."[28] These traits will distinguish him greatly from his son, the feckless Henry VI.

Henry V is not just a shouting head-splitter; Shakespeare shows us a multi-dimensional character, one capable of both heroic display and inner doubt. Henry's depth is especially evident in the scenes on the eve of the Battle of Agincourt. Shakespeare allows us to see both Henry's attention to the detail of the preparation for battle, as he roams through the camp assessing the morale of his men, and the awesome weight of responsibility he feels as king:

Upon the king! let us our lives, our souls,
Our debts, our careful wives,

---

[26] Spiekerman, *Shakespeare's Political Realism,* 125.

[27] Leggatt, *Shakespeare's Political Drama,* 127.

[28] Spiekerman, *Shakespeare's Political Realism,* 150.

Our children and our sins lay on the king!

We must bear all.

Henry V, Act 4, Scene 1

In the end, however, he resolves any doubts and in the face of considerable odds, perhaps as much as five to one, rouses his men to victory. Overhearing talk of the strength of the French, he gives one of the great speeches of the English language:

This story shall the good man teach his son;

And Crispin Crispian [a feast day] shall ne'er go by,

From this day to the ending of the world,

But we in it shall be remember'd;

We few, we happy few, we band of brothers;

For he to-day that sheds his blood with me

Shall be my brother; be he ne'er so vile,

This day shall gentle his condition:

And gentlemen in England now a-bed

Shall think themselves accursed they were not here,

And hold their manhoods cheap whiles any speaks

That fought with us upon Saint Crispin's day.

Henry V, Act 4, Scene 3

Henry is neither reckless nor intimidated by the odds. He has conducted personal reconnaissance of the battlefield, disposed his forces well, understands the ground on which he is going to fight, checked the condition of his troops, and demonstrated his confidence in them and their leaders.

Henry V is not just a capable soldier. He proves equally adept at marshalling support for the dubiously moral[29] invasion of France, protecting himself against internal plotting, and conducting effective international diplomacy.

In the first scene in the play, as the Bishops of Ely and Canterbury weigh the threat to the Church from a bill in parliament aimed at seizing its property, Henry is shown to be deliberately[30] manipulating the Church into both helping to finance and at the same time providing the moral justification for his war:

---

[29] Spiekerman, *Shakespeare's Political Realism,* 131.

[30] Spiekerman, *Shakespeare's Political Realism,* 130.

Canterbury
> My lord, I'll tell you; that self bill is urged,
> Which in the eleventh year of the last king's reign
> Was like, and had indeed against us pass'd,
> But that the scambling and unquiet time
> Did push it out of farther question.

Ely
> But how, my lord, shall we resist it now?

Canterbury
> It must be thought on. If it pass against us,
> We lose the better half of our possession...

Ely
> This would drink deep.

Canterbury
> 'Twould drink the cup and all.

Ely
> But what prevention?

Canterbury
> The king is full of grace and fair regard
> > *Henry V,* Act 1, Scene 1

The church will both justify the war and fund it.

Aware that he is, thanks to his father's deposition of Richard II, the heir to a usurped throne,[31] Henry is sensitive to direct threats to his rule from within the disaffected nobility. His thwarting of an assassination plot in Act 2, Scene 2 is based on good intelligence, cold manipulation of the conspirators, and ruthless execution of the guilty. The King first tricks the conspirators into recommending their own punishment and then pronounces their fate:

King Henry V
> Touching our person seek we no revenge;
> But we our kingdom's safety must so tender,
> Whose ruin you have sought, that to her laws
> We do deliver you. Get you therefore hence,
> Poor miserable wretches, to your death:
>
> > *Henry V,* Act 2, Scene 2

Henry does what is necessary to protect his throne.

---

[31] Spiekerman, *Shakespeare's Political Realism,* 126.

In the wake of the war with France, Henry negotiates a treaty that enhances his stature, and secures, at least temporarily, the English position in France; it also links the two royal families by securing the French King's daughter as his bride. Shakespeare wraps up months of diplomacy in a few lines, demonstrating the completeness of Henry's triumph:

French King
We have consented to all terms of reason.

King Henry V
Is't so, my lords of England?

Westmoreland
The king hath granted every article:
His daughter first, and then in sequel all,
According to their firm proposed natures.

Henry V, Act 5, Scene 2

Of course what Henry wrought through war and diplomacy was not to last. Shakespeare uses the chorus to both honor Henry and forecast the darker things to come:

Chorus
Small time, but in that small most greatly lived
This star of England: Fortune made his sword;
By which the world's best garden be achieved,
And of it left his son imperial lord.
Henry the Sixth, in infant bands crown'd King
Of France and England, did this king succeed;
Whose state so many had the managing,
That they lost France and made his England bleed:

Henry V, Act 5, Epilogue

Shakespeare nevertheless gives Henry V an enviable performance as a leader who, facing potential death and defeat, rises to the occasion. Reading this play, or seeing it performed, presents a complex model of a powerful and capable leader playing many roles, a model that can be used to reflect on the performance of modern leaders.

FAILURE AT THE TOP: *RICHARD II*

...they well deserve to have,
That know the strong'st and surest way to get.

Richard II, Act 3, Scene 3

Powerful leaders play for keeps. Shakespeare captured this in one line by the future King Richard III in *3 Henry VI:* "Priests pray for enemies, but princes kill." In the political world Shakespeare was addressing, the stakes were often life and death for individuals or entire affinities. *Henry V* provides analysts with a model of strong, even heroic, political and military leadership. There is another leadership type, which is at least as interesting from an intelligence standpoint—the weak leader in a key position of power. Shakespeare's Richard II was such a ruler. According to Alexander Leggatt's analysis of the play, Richard is such a bad king that England itself is threatened. [32]

Questions informing this section include: What are the dimensions of leadership failure? What is it like to lose power? What is it like to believe yourself to be in charge, but to actually be failing? What is it like to see yourself a failure, and know it's your fault? What is it like to see your opponent win? How do your supporters see you as you lose? What is it like to usurp a crown? Is "success ever final?"

Much of the story told in Shakespeare's history plays deals with the succession question: Who gets the throne and does he keep it?[33] More broadly the plays are about gaining and losing power. Questions surrounding the security of Elizabeth I's throne and who would succeed her constituted a real-life backdrop for Shakespeare's plays, guaranteeing both interest and relevance. In the two tetralogies of history plays (*1 Henry VI, 2 Henry VI, 3 Henry VI, Richard III; Richard II, 1 Henry IV, 2 Henry IV, Henry V*) Shakespeare provides a wealth of characters and situations, allowing us to see into the cognitive and behavioral elements of the succession situation. Much of *Richard II* is told from within Richard's mind. And what we see is the mind of a failing leader, one who comes to know the full extent of his failure and to understand that he is the cause.

Richard II fails as king in at least three areas: he fails to manage his kingdom, he fails to manage the members of his affinity and he fails to manage himself. These three domains of failure are interrelated, and, in the words of one scholar: "Richard was chiefly a king who fell." [34]

Richard's mismanagement of his kingdom begins early in the play. The king is faced with resolving a problematic dispute between two powerful members of the nobility: Henry Bolingbroke, the Duke of Hereford and son of John of Gaunt, the leader of the Lancastrians; and Thomas Mowbray, the Duke of Norfolk. Richard's mishandling of this affair becomes a crucial element in his loss of the throne. Throughout, Richard is unable to see the effects of his actions on others. [35]

Richard II has an opportunity to resolve the dispute through traditional means by letting it be settled by a duel between the two men. And he initially proposes to let the issue be decided in the tiltyard, the venue for jousting:

---

[32] Leggatt, *Shakespeare's Political Drama*, 56.

[33] Leggatt, *Shakespeare's Political Drama*, ix.

[34] Peter Saccio, *Shakespeare's English Kings: History, Chronicle, and Drama.* (Oxford: Oxford University Press, 2000), 18.

[35] Leggatt, *Shakespeare's Political Drama*, 63.

King Richard II

> At Coventry, upon Saint Lambert's day:
> There shall your swords and lances arbitrate
> The swelling difference of your settled hate:

Richard II, Act 1, Scene 1

Instead he intervenes at the last moment to stop the duel and chooses to exile both men: Bolingbroke temporarily and Mowbray permanently:

King Richard

> For that our kingdom's earth should not be soil'd
> With that dear blood which it hath fostered;
> And for our eyes do hate the dire aspect
> Of civil wounds plough'd up with neighbours' sword;
> Therefore, we banish you our territories:

Richard II, Act 1, Scene 3

Richard's motives here are complicated. On the face of it, he wants to prevent a bloody feud developing between the factions of Bolingbroke and Mowbray. Bolingbroke is the son of John of Gaunt, the Duke of Lancaster, who, although aging, is a political power in his own right. Mowbray is the less powerful Duke of Norfolk. However, it is not so simple. Mowbray, perhaps at the direction of Richard, has been involved in the killing of a member of the nobility opposed to the king. If so, Richard has a clear motive for removing his accomplice from the scene.[36]

Richard also has reason for getting Bolingbroke out of the Kingdom. He sees Bolingbroke as a potential rival and is jealous of his popularity:[37]

King Richard II

> Off goes his bonnet to an oyster-wench;
> A brace of draymen bid God speed him well
> And had the tribute of his supple knee,
> With "Thanks, my countrymen, my loving friends";
> As were our England in reversion his,
> And he our subjects' next degree in hope.

Richard II, Act 1, Scene 4

Richard does show some concern for the potential effects of his actions. He knows that he is making potential enemies, and he has Bolingbroke and Mowbray take an oath that they will never cooperate against the king.

---

[36] Spiekerman, *Shakespeare's Political Realism*, 60.
[37] Spiekerman, *Shakespeare's Political Realism*, 60.

The two men accept their fates, but it is evident Bolingbroke remains a potential political factor, as under normal circumstance he would inherit his father's wealth and position upon his death. And it is here that Richard makes what proves to be a fatal error. Eager for wealth and ignoring well-established norms, he decides to seize John of Gaunt's assets. Informed that John is on his death's bed, Richard proclaims:

King Richard II
Now put it, God, in the physician's mind
To help him to his grave immediately!
The lining of his coffers shall make coats
To deck our soldiers for these Irish wars.
Come, gentlemen, let's all go visit him:
Pray God we may make haste, and come too late!

Richard II, Act 1, Scene 4

Richard is advised against appropriating the possessions of Bolingbroke:

Duke of York
Now, afore God—God forbid I say true!—
If you do wrongfully seize Hereford's [Bolingbroke] rights,
You pluck a thousand dangers on your head,
You lose a thousand well-disposed hearts
And prick my tender patience, to those thoughts
Which honour and allegiance cannot think.

Richard II, Act 2, Scene 1

The king coldly replies:

Think what you will, we seize into our hands
His plate, his goods, his money and his lands.

Richard II, Act 2, Scene 1

This cavalier action strikes at one of the basic social/political norms of the time: that title and possessions passed to the eldest son. It was a fundamental component of the "frame of order" upon which political and social life were built,[38] and an attack upon it threatened not only the individual targeted, but also every man of rank and property in the land. In doing this Richard breaks the system of mutual commitments between the king and his lords, and advances the situation from one of personal antagonism to an eventual threat to the throne.

---

[38] F.R.H. Du Boulay, *An Age of Ambition: English Society in the Late Middle Ages* (New York: The Viking Press, 1970), 128-142.

Henry Bolingbroke was given an issue around which to rally broad support for an armed return to England, if not to seize the throne, at least to reclaim what is rightfully his. He takes advantage of it and sets out on the course that will make him Henry IV.

Richard's difficulties in managing the kingdom are not limited to this particular failure. Shakespeare shows us an increasingly willful leader, no longer heeding sound advice, and creating opposition to his rule as he goes. Shakespeare reveals the discontent with the king spreading across society as important lords discuss the political situation in the wake of Richard's actions against John of Gaunt and his son:

Northumberland
> Now, afore God, 'tis shame such wrongs are borne
> In him, a royal prince, and many more
> Of noble blood in this declining land.
> The king is not himself, but basely led
> By flatterers…

Lord Ross
> The commons hath he pill'd [stripped bare] with grievous taxes
> And quite lost their hearts: the nobles hath he fined
> For ancient quarrels, and quite lost their hearts.

Richard II, Act 2, Scene 1

These men, and others, will rally to Henry Bolingbroke's cause and will participate in the military and political campaign that brings Richard down. And in this dialogue Shakespeare introduces the second leadership failing of Richard II, namely, his inability to control his supporters: "The king is not himself, but basely led by flatterers."

Sir John Bushy, Sir John Bagot, and Sir Henry Green, portrayed as corrupt members of the king's affinity, become lightning rods for Richard's opponents and serve as symbols of his failure to ensure order within his own house. Shakespeare at the end of Act 2, Scene 3, sketches the role of these men as symbols of Richard's failure as a leader. In this scene Henry Bolingbroke has been attempting to convince the Duke of York, one of the king's strongest supporters, to switch sides, and he lays out the next step in his campaign:

Henry Bolingbroke
> But we must win your grace [York] to go with us
> To Bristol castle, which they say is held
> By Bushy, Bagot and their complices,
> The caterpillars of the commonwealth,
> Which I have sworn to weed and pluck away.

Richard II, Act 2, Scene 3

Shakespeare uses the imagery of Bushy and Bagot devouring the garden of England to capture the contempt with which they are held. What is more, these men know they are at risk. In an earlier scene they had openly discussed their situation and likely fate if Boling-broke succeeds:

Green
Besides, our nearness to the king in love
Is near the hate of those love not the king.

Bagot
And that's the wavering commons: for their love
Lies in their purses, and whoso empties them
By so much fills their hearts with deadly hate.

Bushy
Wherein the king stands generally condemn'd.

Bagot
If judgement lie in them, then so do we,
Because we ever have been near the king.

Green
Well, I will for refuge straight to Bristol castle:
The Earl of Wiltshire is already there.

Bushy
Thither will I with you; for little office
The hateful commons will perform for us,
Except like curs to tear us all to pieces.

Richard II, Act 2, Scene 2

Perhaps more important and interesting than Richard's failure to manage the affairs of state or his associates, is his failure to manage himself. Again Shakespeare's portrait of the failing king is not one-dimensional, but for sure Richard falls short on the personal level. We are able to see this failing from three directions: through the perceptions others hold of Richard, through his actions, and from within his own mind.

Not many perceive Richard as a great king, or even an effective one. John of Gaunt points out some of the king's imperfections in Act 2:

John of Gaunt
Methinks I am a prophet new inspired
And thus expiring do foretell of him:
His rash fierce blaze of riot cannot last,
For violent fires soon burn out themselves;
Small showers last long, but sudden storms are short;
He tires betimes [quickly] that spurs too fast betimes;
With eager feeding food doth choke the feeder:

Light [unthinking] vanity, insatiate cormorant,
Consuming means, soon preys upon itself.

Richard II, Act 2, Scene 1

Richard's actions are major evidence of his failing. He exercises bad judgment in embarking on war in Ireland that can only be supported by increased taxes on the people and the land. He is revealed as greedy and mendacious in his seizure of Bolingbroke's inheritance. His personal treatment of John of Gaunt as he nears death is cruel and callous, with the king deriving no little pleasure from Gaunt's passing. The king also appears indecisive and incompetent in his attempt to restore the military and political situation following Bolingbroke's return to England with an army and a seemingly just cause. Richard's moral collapse in the face of mounting difficulties is manifest in Act 3, Scene 2. At first the king, encouraged by others, tries to right himself:

Duke of Aumerle
Comfort, my liege; remember who you are.

King Richard II
I had forgot myself; am I not king?
Awake, thou coward majesty! thou sleepest.
Is not the king's name twenty thousand names?

Richard II, Act 3, Scene 2

But the flood of bad news breaks the king's will:

King Richard II
What say you now? What comfort have we now?
By heaven, I'll hate him everlastingly
That bids me be of comfort any more.
Go to Flint castle: there I'll pine away;
A king, woe's slave, shall kingly woe obey.

Richard II, Act 3, Scene 2

Richard also sees, in own mind, his own failing, and Shakespeare's re-creation of the thought-world of a fading leader is compelling reading. Richard's reaction to the mounting crisis is again illustrative of this as he tells his supporters:

With solemn reverence: throw away respect,
Tradition, form and ceremonious duty,
For you have but mistook me all this while:
I live with bread like you, feel want,
Taste grief, need friends: subjected thus,
How can you say to me, I am a king?

Richard II, Act 3, Scene 2

Soon faced with imminent deposition, Richard's mind is again in turmoil:

King Richard II
> O that I were as great
> As is my grief, or lesser than my name!
> Or that I could forget what I have been,
> Or not remember what I must be now!

> *Richard II,* Act 3, Scene 3

The contrast with Henry V could hardly be greater.

As a ruler there is little that Richard does right, and his descent is a morally and psychologically complex one; but at least part of his fall is due to the rising ambitions of Henry Bolingbroke. Shakespeare shows us the mounting aspirations of Bolingbroke as his ambitions progress from restoration of his property to seizure of the crown. Two passages illustrate this change. In Act 3, Scene 3, Bolingbroke makes his case for support for his cause based on denied rights:

Henry Bolingbroke
> On both his knees doth kiss King Richard's hand
> And sends allegiance and true faith of heart
> To his most royal person, hither come
> Even at his feet to lay my arms and power,
> Provided that my banishment repeal'd
> And lands restored again be freely granted:

> *Richard II,* Act 3, Scene 3

But by Act 4, Scene 1 his supporters are telling him that the crown is his by right. And he believes them, as he proclaims: "In God's name, I'll ascend the regal throne."

Shakespeare contrasts vividly the increasing incapacity of Richard with the vaulting ambition of his emergent rival Bolingbroke. To some extent Richard's great misfortune was to have Henry Bolingbroke as his opponent. Shakespeare also demonstrates that the circumstances under which power is achieved and the character of the successor have much to say about the stability of his success. Bolingbroke's triumph creates conditions of political instability that will plague him as the newly crowned Henry IV, and that will not be finally resolved until Henry Tudor deposes Richard III. Richard II, at the moment of his deposition, points to the mechanisms of instability engendered by the irregular succession process:

> Northumberland, thou ladder wherewithal
> The mounting Bolingbroke ascends my throne...
> -- [39]
> Though he divide the realm and give thee half,
> It is too little, helping him to all;
> And he shall think that thou, which know'st the way

---

[39] Dashed line indicates portion of passage omitted.

To plant unrightful kings, wilt know again,
Being ne'er so little urged, another way
To pluck him headlong from the usurped throne.

Richard II, Act 5, Scene 1

Finally, and perhaps most poignantly, Shakespeare lets us see inside the deposed Richard's mind as he looks back on what might have been and forward to an uncertain fate:

Now sir, the sound that tells what hour it is
Are clamorous groans, which strike upon my heart,
Which is the bell: so sighs and tears and groans
Show minutes, times, and hours: but my time
Runs posting on in Bolingbroke's proud joy,
While I stand fooling here, his Jack o' the clock

Richard II, Act 5, scene 5

Imprisoned by Henry IV, Richard has one last moment of royal behavior as he fights back against the assassins sent to kill him:

King Richard II
That hand shall burn in never-quenching fire
That staggers thus my person. Exton [one of the assassins], thy fierce hand
Hath with the king's blood stain'd the king's own land.
Mount, mount, my soul! thy seat is up on high;
Whilst my gross flesh sinks downward, here to die.
[Dies]

Richard II, Act 5, Scene 5

"THE BIOGRAPHY OF FORCE": *RICHARD III*

Bloody thou art, bloody will be thy end
Richard III, Act 4, Scene 4

Richard III offers a reading in the pure exercise of force. Richard, as Shakespeare portrays him, epitomizes another type of leadership behavior we see today: the ruthless, exhilarating, sometimes pathological, pursuit and exercise of power. King Richard III, as re-created by Shakespeare, provides useful images and metaphors for leaders like Saddam Hussein, who seem in some ways to have stepped up to the highest level of inhumanity, that of the truly evil. Two of the characteristics that made Hitler fundamentally evil were the creativity he exhibited in causing terrible things to happen and the pleasure he derived from it.[40] Saddam seems to fit this profile, as does Shakespeare's *Richard III.*

---

[40] Ron Rosenbaum, *Explaining Hitler: The Search for the Origins of His Evil* (New York: Random House, 1998), 212-216.

Questions of interest to analysts raised by the play include: What is it like to covet the throne? What is it like to be willing to do anything to win it? Can one enjoy oneself in the gaining of it? Can a person be evil and still have admirable qualities? What are the limits on the exercise of power and the use of force? What are the implications of evil at the pinnacle of leadership?

From the first lines of *Richard III*, we are involved in Richard's quest for power, not as remote observers but as intimate witnesses to his thinking. We become complicit to a degree in his thoughts and deeds. Richard enjoys what he does, and on some level we do too: "Richard co-opts us as fellow torturers, sharing guilty pleasures with the added frisson that we may join the victims, if the dominant hunchback detects any failure in our complicity." [41]

Richard III is about power, its acquisition, use, and enjoyment for personal goals, and in a context where the primary actor is largely unconstrained by social or political norms. Shakespeare's Richard is not just another successful pretender to the throne, like Bolingbroke in *Richard II*. Richard is in a class by himself, and he has the tools at his disposal for widespread malevolence. For Richard, even as the Duke of Gloucester, is a powerful political and military figure in his own right. Once seated on the throne, his capacity for mischief only expands.

We first meet Richard in *2 Henry VI* as the Duke of Gloucester. Despite his physical deformity (hunch or "crook" back) he is a skilled and determined combatant in his father's (the Duke of York) cause, and a major instrument in the destruction of the Lancastrians. Midway through *3 Henry VI* Shakespeare reveals to us what is on Richard's mind:

So do I wish the crown, being so far off;

And so I chide the means that keeps me from it;

And so I say, I'll cut the causes off,

> *3 Henry VI*, Act 3, Scene 2

By the end of this play Richard's intentions are even clearer as Shakespeare again opens his mind to us:

I have no brother, I am like no brother;

And this word "love," which graybeards call divine,

Be resident in men like one another

And not in me: I am myself alone.

Clarence, beware; thou keep'st me from the light:

> 3 Henry VI, Act 5, Scene 6

---

[41] Bloom, *Shakespeare*, 71.

To achieve the throne, Richard will exercise force in three domains: the personal, the political, and the military. In all his kingdom there is none to match him until his own actions create opposition forces potent enough to defeat him.

In the opening soliloquy of *Richard III* we are made to understand that Richard appreciates his task and his tools. We see his perceptions of the situation he faces, his objectives, and the means he intends to use to achieve them:

> Why, I, in this weak piping time of peace,
> Have no delight to pass away the time,
> Unless to spy my shadow in the sun
> And descant on mine own deformity:
> And therefore, since I cannot prove a lover,
> To entertain these fair well-spoken days,
> I am determined to prove a villain
> And hate the idle pleasures of these days.
> Plots have I laid, inductions dangerous,
> By drunken prophecies, libels and dreams,
> To set my brother Clarence and the king
> In deadly hate the one against the other:

> *Richard III,* Act 1, Scene 1

Our first glimpse of Richard's ability to wield power is his exercise of his conspiratorial skills to lay the plots that will move his cause ahead. As the play begins he is already moving to eliminate his brother Clarence as a potential successor to King Edward.

An even more intimate use of personal power follows this maneuver against his brother. Richard clearly enjoys the exercise of his powers of psychological domination. For him the application of power is not simply necessary to achieve a goal; it is to be relished in its own right. This is evident in his relationship with Anne, the wife of the Lancastrian Prince Edward, whom Richard has murdered in *3 Henry VI*. Richard's seduction of Anne is purely an exercise in personal power. While Richard's delight is best seen on stage or in the cinema, it still comes through clearly in text. Again Shakespeare shows us Richard's innermost thinking:

> Was ever woman in this humour woo'd?
> Was ever woman in this humour won?
> I'll have her; but I will not keep her long.

> *Richard III,* Act 1, Scene 2

It is manifest that he is going to enjoy the taking.

Richard's conspiratorial power in the political realm is vast and virtually unchecked. The first half of the play is essentially the working out of his plots to attain the throne. At first he operates, essentially alone, spinning a web of lies and deceits that entangles all the principal characters:

Gloucester
> I do the wrong, and first begin to brawl.
> The secret mischiefs that I set abroach
> I lay unto the grievous charge of others...

Richard III, Act 1, Scene 3

Richard rapidly gains adherents, especially the ambitious, although not quite as intelligent or ruthless, Duke of Buckingham. Those who do not side with Richard are either cast aside or removed physically. His sheer exuberance in the working out of his task is breathtaking.

In late medieval England, the acquisition and use of power depended on the careful construction and maintenance of webs of personal allegiance—or, as we have seen, "affinities." As Richard gains adherents, his capacity for more ambitious strokes rises. The combination of the members of his own affinity with the powerful Duke of Buckingham and other lords provides Richard the political and military clout he needs to contest the succession.

The 1995 cinema version of *Richard III* shows the energy and excitement of the plotters to great advantage.[42] Richard, played by the incomparable Ian McKellen, and his cohorts are shown marauding through the English political system like a band of highly evolved predators. They buffalo, bluster, and bamboozle their way to the throne, killing where they have to, and hugely enjoying themselves. Roaring around London in their powerful cars and fascist-style uniforms, they almost seem like upper class Nazis, or even the former ruling elite of Iraq. The scenes of Richard as king dealing with his subordinates are jarringly familiar for those who have watched videotape of Saddam presiding publicly.

Once in power, on the throne, conspiracy and manipulation work less well for Richard. Attempts to use Buckingham to further the murder of Edward's heirs go awry. Edward IV's queen Elizabeth is unwilling to sacrifice her daughter on Richard's marriage bed to retain her privileged position. Ultimately he will have to resort to pure force—military power—to deal with the emerging threats to his crown. In this arena he is not without skill, however, and even with key supporters deserting him he proves a formidable commander.

Like some modern dictators, Richard is not without admirable qualities. He is decisive, and he is courageous. Richard's power of decision is shown at multiple points in the play. In Act 4, Scene 3 we see Richard at his best, responding to threats from multiple enemies and directions:

> Then fiery expedition be my wing,
> Jove's Mercury, and herald for a king!
> Come, muster men: my counsel is my shield;

---

[42] United Artists Pictures, *Richard III*, 1995.

We must be brief when traitors brave the field.

Richard III, Act 4, Scene 2

At the end of the play Richard shows his personal courage in the Battle of Bosworth. When one of his loyalists pleads with him to withdraw, the king responds, famously:

Slave, I have set my life upon a cast,
And I will stand the hazard of the die:

Richard III, Act 4, Scene 2

Richard goes down fighting, not running.

Was Richard evil? Is this even a relevant question for an analyst? Both Richard's analytical powers and his capacity for evil are displayed in Act 4, Scene 2 as he calculates his next move:

I must be married to my brother's daughter,
Or else my kingdom stands on brittle glass.
Murder her brothers, and then marry her!
Uncertain way of gain! But I am in
So far in blood that sin will pluck on sin:
Tear-falling pity dwells not in this eye.

Richard III, Act 4, Scene 2

He is shocking, he knows it, and he enjoys it. In this play Shakespeare gives us a sense of intimacy with evil that other reporting cannot provide. Watching, or reading, *Richard III* you have the sensation of being in, or close to, a mental world like that of Saddam Hussein.

Richard, again as Shakespeare has chosen to portray him, is a high-ranking criminal and sociopath. For him the ends justify the means ("I'm in so far in blood, that sin will pluck on sin"). In the telling of the story, we are allowed to see the consequences of evil at the top. Much of what Richard does, while advancing his goals on one level, is simultaneously undermining them on another. The murders, broken promises, threats, and victimizations create a growing body of opposition to his rule, one that becomes powerful enough to defeat him when the circumstances are right, although even here Shakespeare draws the situation in a nuanced way. It is not so clear that Richard will lose at Bosworth Field. Ironically, it takes a foreign-supported invasion and treachery, by the powerful Stanley affinity, to defeat him. And at the end he still has his stalwarts who are willing to die with him.

Shakespeare has given us a particular re-creation of Richard III. Some historians argue that the historical Richard was actually quite a nice fellow. Nevertheless, throughout this play Richard is depicted as multi-dimensional. He is not a cardboard villain. Shakespeare gives us both the "evil" Richard and the admirable one, demonstrating that leaders are difficult subjects of analysis, elusive of easy categorization, and those that are both evil and competent can be formidable. Richard's complexity should make us conscious of the difference between an evil or disagreeable target and an easy one, and cognizant of the actual depths of behavior and personality that lie behind a foreign leader's image, and that may not emerge in intelligence reporting.

Richard, like Saddam, dominates. All of the other characters in the play are foils for his thoughts and actions. Even in defeat Richard towers over the other participants in the struggle. The only character with anything like his presence is Queen Margaret, the wife of Henry VI, who casts curses like Richard spins plots. She is a central figure in the three parts of *Henry VI* and the Wars of the Roses, and her powers will be explored later in this paper.

CIVIL WAR: 1, 2, 3 HENRY VI

> I will stir up in England some black storm
> Shall blow ten thousand souls to heaven or hell;
> And this fell tempest shall not cease to rage
> Until the golden circuit [crown] on my head...

2 Henry VI, Act 3, Scene 1

Civil Wars and related phenomena draw much attention from political and military analysts. The complex environments from which they emerge, the role of personalities, and the unintended consequences they bring, are subjects of great intelligence interest. Shakespeare's three plays built around the England of Henry VI raise challenging questions for all analysts involved with such events: What are the key dynamics of a civil war? How does violence expand? How does violence become personal? How does the use of violence evolve as a civil war emerges? How is violence justified, to the self and to the group? What kinds of behavior and actions does it produce? What do the leaders see as the civil war process begins and progresses? What do they do in response? Since England had a significant history of civil conflict, Shakespeare had a wealth of material to work with. The enduring analytical questions raised by the Wars of the Roses, the civil war of 15th Century England, make his "case studies" relevant to analysts today.

A central element in the *Henry VI* trilogy is the expansion of violence. What starts out as personal ambition finishes as full-blown warfare between rival dynastic houses, with tens of thousands of troops in the field, extended military campaigns, and major battles. Shakespeare furnishes us with a model of how a personal contest for power can become a civil war.

In the initial act of *1 Henry VI* Shakespeare sets out the forces that will be in contention in the wake of Henry V's death. Opportunity is provided by Henry VI's youth (an infant of nine months), and the plot is driven forward by the desire of ambitious men to exploit this. As related by Shakespeare, the forces contending around the throne are: the old order represented by the Duke of Gloucester, the church represented by the Bishop of Winchester, and several personally ambitious nobles. These men will bring Henry V's "perfect garden" to wrack and ruin and ensure the loss of England's lands in France. Shakespeare develops for us the enormous costs, personal and national, of unconstrained political ambition.

Shakespeare also reveals the complexity of this process of decline into civil war. What we see unfold is not a simple contest for influence or power by two sides but a multi-faceted one, in which temporary alliances are made, personal commitments broken, and the quest for political advantage overrules social and political norms. Witchcraft, murder and treason are all brought to play.

One of the first conflicts developed is between the Duke of Gloucester, the lord protector during Henry VI's minority and representative of the old order, and Winchester, representing the political presence of the church:

Gloucester

The church! where is it? Had not churchmen pray'd,
His [Henry V] thread of life had not so soon decay'd:
None do you like but an effeminate prince,
Whom, like a school-boy, you may over-awe.

Bishop of Winchester

Gloucester, whate'er we like, thou art protector
And lookest to command the prince and realm.
Thy wife is proud; she holdeth thee in awe,
More than God or religious churchmen may.

1 Henry VI, Act 1, Scene 1

Shakespeare displays for us not only the political (state vs. church) rivalry between Gloucester and Winchester, but also the deep personal animosity between the two men that exacerbates the political conflict. A few lines later, as Winchester speaks in an aside, we are able to see his true political ambition:

Bishop of Winchester

Each hath his place and function to attend:
I am left out; for me nothing remains.
But long I will not be Jack out of office:
The king from Eltham I intend to steal
And sit at chiefest stern of public weal.

1 Henry VI, Act 1, Scene 1

As the play progresses, words become deeds, and in Act 1, Scene 3 the first violence between the factions of the duke and the bishop breaks out in the streets of London. Winchester now defines Gloucester as a mortal enemy:

Bishop of Winchester

Abominable Gloucester, guard thy head;
For I intend to have it ere long.

1 Henry VI, Act 1, Scene 3

To this conflict Shakespeare adds the quest for power of ambitious nobles, both in dynastic terms and in terms of personal influence. With the exception of Gloucester, none of these people is personally admirable. The author cautions us against too easy an identification with the characters in a power struggle; as in Lebanon during its civil war, Christians are not necessarily the "good guys" and honorable words can cover rank ambition.

Act 2, Scene 4 introduces the beginning of the central political conflict that dominates the first tetralogy (*1,2,3 Henry VI,* and *Richard III*), the contest between the houses of York and Lancaster. Over the course of the four plays, this emerges as the Wars of the Roses. Shakespeare develops this slowly at first with relatively minor incidents, and then with gathering speed and expanding violence.

A legal dispute between Richard Plantagenet (York) and the Earl of Somerset (Lancaster) sets events in motion. When Somerset loses a legal appeal he resorts to threats of violence:

Richard Plantagenet
     Now, Somerset, where is your argument?

Somerset
     Here in my scabbard, meditating that
     Shall dye your white rose in a bloody red.

          1 Henry VI, Act 2, Scene

In a scene of escalating taunts and personal insults Richard and Somerset become the bitterest of enemies. Shakespeare uses the powerful image of red or white roses to depict the taking of sides:

Somerset
     Ah, thou [Richard] shalt find us ready for thee still;
     And know us by these colours for thy foes,
     For these my friends in spite of thee shall wear.

Richard Plantagenet
     And, by my soul, this pale and angry rose,
     As cognizance of my blood-drinking hate,
     Will I for ever and my faction wear,
     Until it wither with me to my grave
     Or flourish to the height of my degree

          1 Henry VI, Act 2, Scene 4

In the space of a few lines two powerful and deeply divided factions are created. Given that the basis of armed power at that time was the number of retainers that each figure could muster, the military basis for the coming war was also being established. Early street fighting between members of the factions portends the later pitched battles of the Wars of the Roses.

In the last acts of *1 Henry VI* the third set of forces that will drive England into civil war is introduced: Suffolk's ambition to be the principal advisor to the king, as complicated by his emergent relationship with Margaret of Anjou, one of the most formidable of Shakespeare's female characters. Suffolk is an early supporter of Somerset but he plays his own game, aiming not to sit on the throne but to stand next to it.

We first notice Suffolk in the rose selection scene as he lines up with the Lancastrians; but by Act 5, Scene 3, he is emerging as a contender for influence. Here we witness him in his first encounter with Margaret of Anjou, and it is easy to see that this will be a key relationship:

Margaret
Say, Earl of Suffolk—if thy name be so—
What ransom must I pay before I pass?
For I perceive I am thy prisoner.

Suffolk [aside]
How canst thou tell she will deny thy suit,
Before thou make a trial of her love?

Margaret
Why speak'st thou not? what ransom must I pay?

Suffolk [aside]
She's beautiful, and therefore to be woo'd;
She is a woman, therefore to be won.

1 Henry VI, Act 5, Scene 3

Suffolk arranges for her to become Henry VI's queen, although that development does not deter what soon emerges, in Shakespeare's telling, as a passionate relationship.

Margaret's eventual marriage to Henry VI is one of the key developments that intensify the conflict; increasingly she will provide the ambition, leadership, and commanding presence that the King lacks. In the words of one scholar: ...Margaret, while playing the shadow role of queen, will control the substance of power in the second and third parts of the play. [43]

Shakespeare makes clear that much of this descent into violence is due to the weakness of the king, both his personal weakness[44] and the political weakness of his house founded on the usurpation of Richard II's throne by Henry Bolingbroke. But the author suggests as

---

[43] Michael Hattaway, Introduction to *The First Part of King Henry VI,* The New Cambridge Shakespeare, ed. Michael Hattaway (Cambridge: Cambridge University Press, 1990), 28.

[44] Leggatt, *Shakespeare's Political Drama,* 24-25.

well that it was not simply a weak king that is to blame, pointing to personal ambition, sexual desire, and the violation of political and social norms as instrumental. The dramatist illuminates for us the complex web of causes, motives and emotions that stoke a civil war. Disentangling these in an ongoing or developing civil conflict can be a formidable challenge for analysts.

In *2 Henry VI,* Shakespeare offers us an escalating and expanding internal conflict in which the contestants begin to appeal to outside forces for assistance. The stability of the state is shaken, and England suffers irretrievable territorial losses in France through poor diplomacy and military failure abetted by personal rivalries. Shakespeare instructs us that these are some the consequences of civil war.

Political violence increases as factions solidify and extreme measures are taken, including treason, murder and resort to witchcraft, a kind of appeal to outside forces. Margaret becomes Queen and rapidly emerges as the real power. The loss of territory in France, through Suffolk's questionable marriage diplomacy and contention over accountability for military defeats drives the contestants for power into still deeper conflict.

In the first act of *2 Henry VI,* Shakespeare further develops the conflicts established in *1 Henry VI.* While the King and the growing faction of Suffolk are most pleased with the marriage, Gloucester and his faction are appalled at the terms and the rising influence of Suffolk and the Queen. Reading the terms of the marriage contract, Gloucester is dismayed:

> O peers of England, shameful is this league!
> Fatal this marriage, cancelling your fame,
> Blotting your names from books of memory,
> Razing the characters of your renown,
> Defacing monuments of conquer'd France,
> Undoing all, as all had never been!

> *2 Henry VI,* Act 1, Scene 1

And Gloucester's ally York takes a swipe at Suffolk who has been raised to the rank of Duke:

York
> For Suffolk's duke, may he be suffocate,
> That dims the honour of this warlike isle!

> 2 Henry VI, Act 1, Scene 1

Shakespeare illustrates the intricate, even intimate, nature of intense competition for power and influence, revealing the divisions and undercurrents that exist within the factions. First Somerset, of Suffolk's faction, raises concerns about Cardinal Beaufort:

Somerset
> Cousin of Buckingham, though Humphrey's [Gloucester] pride
> And greatness of his place be grief to us,

Yet let us watch the haughty cardinal:
His insolence is more intolerable
Than all the princes in the land beside:
If Gloucester be displaced, he'll be protector

2 *Henry VI*, Act 1, Scene 1

Then it is the turn of Gloucester's faction, as York reveals his own ambitions:

Then will I raise aloft the milk-white rose,
With whose sweet smell the air shall be perfumed;
And in my standard bear the arms of York
To grapple with the house of Lancaster;
And, force perforce, I'll make him [Henry VI] yield the crown,
Whose bookish rule hath pull'd fair England down

2 *Henry VI*, Act 1, Scene 1

In the lines preceding those above, Shakespeare exposes the cognitive process by which York justifies his treason to his king and Gloucester:

The peers agreed, and Henry was well pleased
To change two dukedoms for a duke's fair daughter.
I cannot blame them all: what is't to them?
'Tis thine they give away, and not their own...

So York must sit and fret and bite his tongue,
While his own lands are bargain'd for and sold....

Anjou and Maine both given unto the French!
Cold news for me, for I had hope of France,
Even as I have of fertile England's soil.

2 *Henry VI*, Act 1, Scene 1

We see York's perceptions of the situation, how he defines it, and then what he intends to do about it. We enter into the realm of his "intentions."

Through the rest of this play, Shakespeare concentrates on the intense plotting among the principal characters, setting the stage for the decisive struggle between the Houses of York and Lancaster. The escalating rivalry ultimately leads to the ruin of Gloucester, his wife Eleanor, Suffolk, and Beaufort (Winchester). All but Eleanor die violent deaths plotted by their opponents, and her fate—disgrace and exile for practicing witchcraft—is hardly better. This thinning out of those competing for influence focuses the struggle on those who want to keep (Margaret) or gain (York) the crown and their affinities.

While Margaret works to strengthen her husband's hold on the throne, and thereby her own power, York stirs rebellion and moves toward outright insurrection. In Act 2, Scene 2, he seeks to persuade his allies, Warwick and Salisbury, that he has a legitimate claim to the throne:

York

Now, my good Lords of Salisbury and Warwick,
Our simple supper ended, give me leave
In this close walk to satisfy myself,
In craving your opinion of my title,
Which is infallible, to England's crown.

Salisbury

My lord, I long to hear it at full.

Warwick

Sweet York, begin: and if thy claim be good,
The Nevils [Warwick's family] are thy subjects to command.

2 Henry VI, Act 2, Scene 2

York is successful, but he knows that it will require conspiracy and war to achieve his goal, and that proves no deterrent:

York

We thank you, lords. But I am not your king
Till I be crown'd and that my sword be stain'd
With heart-blood of the house of Lancaster;
And that's not suddenly to be perform'd,
But with advice and silent secrecy.

2 Henry VI, Act 2, Scene 2

York also knows that he must especially maintain the support of the powerful Warwick. Shakespeare lays out the bargain between the two men:

Warwick

My heart assures me that the Earl of Warwick
Shall one day make the Duke of York a king.

York

And, Nevil [Warwick], this I do assure myself:
Richard [York] shall live to make the Earl of Warwick
The greatest man in England but the king.

2 Henry VI, Act 2, Scene 2

Together York and Warwick represent a power capable of challenging the king, and the mutual commitment between the two men signals civil war between the houses of York and Lancaster.

All does not go York's way however, as the Queen and her faction are able to remove York from the immediate political stage by having him sent to Ireland. But York is able to turn this to his own advantage, using the opportunity to build his own military strength, and to lay plots against the king:

> Whiles I in Ireland nourish a mighty band,
> I will stir up in England some black storm
> Shall blow ten thousand souls to heaven or hell;
> And this fell tempest shall not cease to rage
> Until the golden circuit [crown] on my head,

> *2 Henry VI,* Act 3, Scene 1

What York does is to initiate Cade's Rebellion, which eventually comes to threaten the throne. That York is willing to contemplate such measures shows the depth of his ambition. Shakespeare also exposes the extent of York's cynicism in a soliloquy:

> Say that he [Cade] thrive, as 'tis great like he will,
> Why, then from Ireland come I with my strength
> And reap the harvest which that rascal sow'd;
> For Humphrey [Gloucester] being dead, as he shall be,
> And Henry put apart, the next for me.

> *2 Henry VI,* Act 3, Scene 1

The ultimate failure of Cade's rebellion and Margaret' success, along with her new ally Somerset, in holding the throne for her husband, sets the stage for the first outright battle of the Wars of the Roses, at Saint Alban's. This is a victory for the Yorkist forces. Although the Lancastrians are routed they are not destroyed, with the King and Queen escaping.

Shakespeare uses two mechanisms to drive the escalation of violence that is to come in the wake of St. Alban's. The killing of key Lancastrian officers, including Somerset and Clifford, sets the stage for even greater personal violence as revenge is sought and gained. He also introduces characters that will carry the conflict forward: York's sons, including Richard of Gloucester, and Clifford's son, who will prove a determined foe of the House of York. The relatively simple personal rivalries of the first acts of *1 Henry VI,* have become a full-blown civil war extending across generations. All of this is fully realized in *3 Henry VI.*

In *3 Henry VI* the courses of action set in the first two plays follow their paths. The civil war becomes increasingly bloody as both sides have trouble gaining decisive advantage and holding it. Attempts at political compromise fail. Loyalty is dishonored as key players switch sides; as one authority put it, "in the world of Henry VI loyalty is the exception, not the rule."[45] The atrocities pile up with echoes of modern civil conflicts. Shakespeare depicts the results of personal ambition carried to its ultimate conclusion. The Wars of the Roses tear England apart.

Shakespeare depicts the deepening violence of the civil war in several scenes. The play opens with the Yorkists celebrating Henry VI's defeat at Saint Alban's and their own personal exploits in killing their foes:

Edward

Lord Stafford's father, Duke of Buckingham,

Is either slain or wounded dangerously;

I cleft his beaver [helmet] with a downright blow:

That this is true, father, behold his blood.

Montague

And, brother, here's the Earl of Wiltshire's blood,

Whom I encounter'd as the battles join'd.

Richard

Speak thou for me and tell them what I did.

[Throwing down Somerset's head]

York

Richard hath best deserved of all my sons.

But is your grace dead, my Lord of Somerset?

3 Henry VI, Act 1, Scene 1

They all have rather enjoyed it. Later, however, in a scene where a father kills his son and a son kills his father in battle, Shakespeare portrays the personal tragedies the civil war is imposing on the English people. [46]

In fact the conflict becomes more generalized as the Lancastrains resort to scorched earth policies and seek help from France and Scotland. Uncharacteristically the meek and pious Henry VI himself declares his willingness to do whatever it takes to hold the throne:

King Henry VI

Think'st thou that I will leave my kingly throne,

Wherein my grandsire and my father sat?

No: first shall war unpeople this my realm;

Ay, and their colours, often borne in France,

And now in England to our heart's great sorrow,

Shall be my winding-sheet.

3 Henry VI, Act 1 Scene 1

[45] Milton Crane, Introduction to *Henry VI: Part Three,* The Signet Classic Shakespeare (New York: Penguin, 1968) Stanley, xxviii.

[46] Leggatt, *Shakespeare's Political Drama,* 20.

Loyalties crumble throughout the play. York's son Clarence switches sides several times, earning a reputation for treachery, which will be paid off in *Richard III*. Ultimately, after York's eldest son Edward assumes the throne, even Warwick will prove disloyal.

In fact the later part of the play begins to reveal the internal rivalries within the house of York that will bring it down. Richard and Clarence have their own ambitions, and Richard begins to plot almost immediately against his other brother, the newly crowned Edward IV. In Act 3, Scene 2, Shakespeare reveals Richard working it out in his mind:

[Richard]
> I can add colours to the chameleon,
> Change shapes with Proteus for advantages,
> And set the murderous Machiavel to school.
> Can I do this, and cannot get a crown?
> Tut, were it farther off, I'll pluck it down

> *3 Henry VI,* Act 3, Scene 2

Richard, in keeping with the deepening conflict, has made the transition from waging honorable war to pursuing armed ambition. He will be able to break all the rules of his society because all the rules have already been broken. What constituted the medieval "frame of order," or the existing political rules of the game, had been well and truly shattered. All of this seems very current.

Over the course of the three plays Shakespeare illustrates how—in the face of unrestrained ambition—political, social, and personal norms are violated. Margaret actually enjoys the killing of her bitter opponent York:

Queen Margaret
> Off with his head, and set it on York gates;
> So York may overlook the town of York.

> *3 Henry VI,* Act 1 Scene 4

And he vividly demonstrates the results in terms of the personal and national costs of civil war. He also lays bare the cognitive processes by which the principal characters, in particular York, convince themselves and others of the rightness of their actions. Most of these people do not see themselves as evil. They are upholding some value. They can justify their actions as either necessary or moral. Only in *Richard III* do we get to see a character that is truly evil, one who needs no justifications.

Direct contact with momentous events is difficult to achieve from typical intelligence reporting. The three parts of *Henry VI* are loaded with images, metaphors and meaning for analysts. They graphically portray a civil war, from its early roots in the political ambitions of a few men and women to the collapse of civil society and widespread conflict. Shakespeare presents us very powerful images illuminating what it means to be caught up in such developments. Reading the three parts of *Henry VI* is not a sterile exercise. It is a journey into human behavior under extreme political, moral, and personal circumstances.

TO PLOT A COUP: JULIUS CAESAR

Such men as he be never at heart's ease
Whiles they behold a greater than themselves,
And therefore are they very dangerous.

Julius Caesar, Act 1, Scene 2

A move to unseat a standing ruler or leadership group can be a momentous action. Even a failed coup is capable of producing far-reaching and unanticipated consequences. For Shakespeare and his high-ranking audience a sudden change of leadership was a real possibility, with potentially dire results. For intelligence analysts, *Julius Caesar* raises many pertinent questions about the processes of a coup and especially the behavior of individuals caught up in one: When is a coup justified? What rationalizations are employed? When is the right time? How do the plotters see one another? How does opposition arise? What are the internal dynamics? What is the range of behaviors among the principals? What are the consequences, intended and unintended?

A sudden move by a band of insiders to topple a government has an inherent subject appeal to analysts. A coup can combine shock, uncertainty, instability, violent action, and unforeseen results in ways that other political events do not. Shakespeare gives us all of this in *Julius Caesar.* And he gives it to us primarily from the perspective of the key conspirators and their opponents. We see not only what they see, but also what they think, and how their perceptions and thoughts connect to the action of the coup and its outcomes.

Perhaps the first question about a coup is why do those mounting it feel the need to do so? It is usually uncertain, and often risky. Shakespeare provides us insight into some of the motivation and thought processes involved. In the first act, second scene we see Brutus expressing his own uncertainty about plotting against Caesar to the lead conspirator Cassius:

Cassius,
Be not deceived: if I have veil'd my look,
I turn the trouble of my countenance
Merely upon myself. Vexed I am
Of late with passions of some difference,
Conceptions only proper to myself,
Which give some soil perhaps to my behaviors;
But let not therefore my good friends be grieved—
Among which number, Cassius, be you one—
Nor construe any further my neglect,
Than that poor Brutus, with himself at war,
Forgets the shows of love to other men.

Julius Caesar, Act 1, Scene 2

Cassius, needing Brutus' support, sees an opening and seeks to persuade him that Caesar intends to become king, posing a threat to all their freedoms:

> Why, man, he doth bestride the narrow world
> Like a Colossus, and we petty men
> Walk under his huge legs and peep about
> To find ourselves dishonourable graves.
> Men at some time are masters of their fates:
> The fault, dear Brutus, is not in our stars,
> But in ourselves, that we are underlings.

> *Julius Caesar*, Act 1, Scene 2

Cassius is successful in moving Brutus closer to a decision to move against Caesar. He understands his target and sets out on an "information warfare" campaign with Brutus as its target:

> [Cassius Aside]
> I will this night,
> In several hands, in at his windows throw,
> As if they came from several citizens,
> Writings all tending to the great opinion
> That Rome holds of his name; wherein obscurely
> Caesar's ambition shall be glanced at:
> And after this let Caesar seat him sure;
> For we will shake him, or worse days endure.

> *Julius Caesar*, Act 1, Scene 2

Cassius has measured his target well, and Brutus soon convinces himself that Caesar must go:

> Fashion it thus; that what he is, augmented,
> Would run to these and these extremities:
> And therefore think him as a serpent's egg
> Which, hatch'd, would, as his kind, grow mischievous,
> And kill him in the shell.

> *Julius Caesar*, Act 2, Scene 1

Shakespeare takes us through a series of dialogues and soliloquies that lay out the cognitive process of Brutus committing to Cassius' enterprise. Brutus, fed by Cassius' clever campaign, builds ("Fashion it thus") a rationalization for a coup, even though he knows Caesar has done nothing yet to justify his assassination.[47] We are able to see this process as it unfolds in Brutus' mind.

---

[47] Leggatt, *Shakespeare's Political Drama*, 144.

Shakespeare also shows us other conspirators committing to the enterprise. Some, like Cassius have worked it out in detail, and Shakespeare gives ample indication that Cassius is plotting on multiple levels. Others, like Casca, seem swept up in the drama of the game. The conspirators are apparently willing to take risks and commit murder, ostensibly on the basis of no more than the belief that Caesar will be corrupt.

Perhaps more importantly, Shakespeare is demonstrating the complexity of motives in a coup both at the individual and group levels. Casca is relatively simple; Brutus and Cassius are much deeper. We also are able to observe a phenomenon evident in other coups: that of individuals moving along a spectrum of commitment at different paces. Cassius is fully committed, at least from the beginning of the play; but others, especially Brutus, must be brought along.

In any coup timing is important, and in *Julius Caesar* we can see this. From the beginning of the plot there is a clear sense of urgency, as the conspirators feel the pressure to act before Caesar is made king. Shakespeare begins to convey this sense of urgency in the second scene of the first act where, as Cassius and Brutus discuss whether or not a coup is justified, they hear the crowd shouting and express their concern that Caesar has already been crowned:

Brutus
    What means this shouting? I do fear, the people
    Choose Caesar for their king.

Cassius
    Ay, do you fear it?
    Then must I think you would not have it so.

Later the conspirators learn that Caesar will be crowned the next day, giving increased urgency to the plot. In addition, the plot runs the risk of discovery. Caesar is warned early (Act 1, Scene 2) that he faces danger. In Act 2 Scene 3 he is given specific warning of the plot including the names of the conspirators:

Artemidorus

    Caesar, beware of Brutus; take heed of Cassius;
    come not near Casca; have an eye to Cinna, trust not
    Trebonius: mark well Metellus Cimber: Decius Brutus
    loves thee not: thou hast wronged Caius Ligarius.
    There is but one mind in all these men, and it is
    bent against Caesar. If thou beest not immortal,
    look about you: security gives way to conspiracy.

The conspirators need to act before Caesar is crowned and before they are rolled up. Their timing is also affected by Caesar's schedule. They know he will be in public and precisely where on the Ides of March.

Any conspiracy is made up of a complex set of personalities, and in Julius Caesar we are able to see this and how this complexity shapes the coup and its aftermath. Cassius' band is not of "one mind." Shakespeare provides clear images of both what they think and what others think of them. Caesar, already suspicious of Cassius, provides a clear image of a suspected conspirator:

> I do not know the man I should avoid
> So soon as that spare Cassius…
> --
> Such men as he be never at heart's ease
> Whiles they behold a greater than themselves,
> And therefore are they very dangerous.

> *Julius Caesar,* Act 1, Scene 2

Cassius provides his view of the conspirator Casca:

> You are dull, Casca, and those sparks of life
> That should be in a Roman you do want,
> Or else you use not. You look pale and gaze
> And put on fear and cast yourself in wonder,
> To see the strange impatience of the heavens:

> *Julius Caesar,* Act 1, Scene 3

And Casca and Cassius weigh Brutus as an asset for the conspiracy:

Casca
> O, he sits high in all the people's hearts:
> And that which would appear offence in us,
> His countenance, like richest alchemy,
> Will change to virtue and to worthiness.

Cassius
> Him and his worth and our great need of him
> You have right well conceited.

> *Julius Caesar,* Act 1, Scene 3

Brutus himself holds strong opinions of other potential conspirators. As Cicero is discussed Brutus makes his feelings clear:

> O, name him not: let us not break [involve] with him;
> For he will never follow any thing
> That other men begin.

> *Julius Caesar,* Act 2, Scene 1

As the conspirators arrive at his house, Brutus reveals his view of the collective enterprise:

They are the faction. O conspiracy,
Shamest thou to show thy dangerous brow by night,
When evils are most free? O, then by day
Where wilt thou find a cavern dark enough
To mask thy monstrous visage? Seek none, conspiracy;
Hide it in smiles and affability:

Julius Caesar, Act 2, Scene 1

These scenes suggest the range of personalities within the plot, the diverse perceptions the plotters have of one another, and potential lines of cleavage in the conspiracy. Clearly this is not a selfless "band of brothers." They are using one another. In contemporary coup situations, detail and nuance of this nature can be undetectable, giving the outward appearance of a solid block of actors moving in unison. Analysts should be sensitive to this kind of nuance and reflect it in their assessments.

Once the coup is underway what happens, and what are the consequences? One of the first processes evident as the coup unfolds is its tendency to expand to include more members and more targets. As the conspirators meet on the eve of the coup they discuss who should be killed along with Caesar. Cassius favors getting rid of Mark Antony, but Brutus argues against it, trying to limit the violence:

Our course will seem too bloody, Caius Cassius,
To cut the head off and then hack the limbs,
Like wrath in death and envy afterwards;
For Antony is but a limb of Caesar:
Let us be sacrificers, but not butchers, Caius.

Julius Caesar, Act 2, Scene 1

Another process evident in the play is the plot's accelerating momentum. This is apparent in the rush of events—discussions, deceptions, meetings—the falling into place of key elements, and the gathering of support. The plot rapidly gathers speed and comes to a head. Again this mirrors contemporary situations. Whatever the preparatory time, at some point a coup shifts into high tempo.

The plot climaxes with Caesar's assassination, and at first the conspirators seem to have won. They immediately try to stabilize the situation and ensure that their explanation of what happened is put out to the public:

Cinna
    Liberty! Freedom! Tyranny is dead!
    Run hence, proclaim, cry it about the streets.

Cassius
    Some to the common pulpits, and cry out
    "Liberty, freedom, and enfranchisement"!

Brutus
> People and senators, be not affrighted;
> Fly not; stand stiff: ambition's debt is paid.

Julius Caesar, Act 3, Scene 1

But the results are not what the plotters expected, and Shakespeare gives us a lesson in unintended consequences. Most important of these consequences is the rapid emergence of organized resistance led by Mark Antony.

Brutus' inability to weigh people properly, first evidenced in his failure to understand Cassius, and second in his failure to understand himself, has led Brutus to underestimate Antony. Brutus not only does not agree to kill Antony, but in the opening moments of the coup he also gives Antony a chance to rally Caesar's supporters. Just as Cassius persuaded Brutus that Caesar had to go, Antony persuades Brutus that Caesar needs a proper send off. Brutus, believing that he is the master of the situation and of Antony, agrees, despite Cassius' misgivings. This is a colossal error:

Cassius
> Brutus, a word with you.

[Aside to Brutus]
> You know not what you do: do not consent
> That Antony speak in his funeral:
> Know you how much the people may be moved
> By that which he will utter?

Brutus
> By your pardon;
> I will myself into the pulpit first,
> And show the reason of our Caesar's death:
> What Antony shall speak, I will protest
> He speaks by leave and by permission,
> And that we are contented Caesar shall
> Have all true rites and lawful ceremonies.
> It shall advantage more than do us wrong.

Julius Caesar, Act 3, scene 1

For a leader of a dangerous enterprise Brutus proves an inept judge of men. As one German general said of the failed July 1944 bomb plot to kill Hitler, "This was not the way to go about it." The sought-after political "precision strike" becomes a civil war.

Standing alone over Caesar's corpse, Antony shows where he stands on the coup and assassination:

> O, pardon me, thou bleeding piece of earth,
> That I am meek and gentle with these butchers!

Thou art the ruins of the noblest man
That ever lived in the tide of times.
Woe to the hand that shed this costly blood!

Julius Caesar, Act 3, Scene 1

Antony goes on in the same soliloquy to forecast the second major unintended consequence of the coup, the rapid emergence of instability and the descent into civil war:

Over thy wounds now do I prophesy…

A curse shall light upon the limbs of men;
Domestic fury and fierce civil strife
Shall cumber all the parts of Italy…

And Caesar's spirit, ranging for revenge,
With Ate by his side come hot from hell,
Shall in these confines with a monarch's voice
Cry 'Havoc,' and let slip the dogs of war;

Julius Caesar, Act 3, Scene 1

Antony of course is one of the principal agents of the onset and spread of violence. In Alexander Leggatt's words: "Brutus wanted a tight, clear, finished action. Antony has broken the play open and set history going in new, unpredictable directions."[48] As Caesar's body is cooling Antony is alerting his ally Octavius to what has happened. Through skillful rhetoric he turns the people against the conspirators:

Antony
  Moreover, he [Caesar] hath left you all his walks,
  His private arbours and new-planted orchards,
  On this side Tiber; he hath left them you,
  And to your heirs for ever, common pleasures,
  To walk abroad, and recreate yourselves.
  Here was a Caesar! when comes such another?

First Citizen
  Never, never. Come, away, away!
  We'll burn his body in the holy place,
  And with the brands fire the traitors' houses.
  Take up the body.

Second Citizen
  Go fetch fire.

---

[48] Leggatt, *Shakespeare's Political Drama*, 158.

Third Citizen
    Pluck down benches.

Fourth Citizen
    Pluck down forms, windows, any thing.
    [Exeunt Citizens with the body]

Antony
    Now let it work. Mischief, thou art afoot,
    Take thou what course thou wilt!

Julius Caesar, Act 3, Scene 2

With the arrival of Octavius in Rome, Antony quickly begins to organize the opposition. As for the conspirators, Shakespeare gives us a brilliant image of a failed coup:

Servant
    I heard him [Octavius] say, Brutus and Cassius
    Are rid like madmen through the gates of Rome.

Antony
    Belike [perhaps] they had some notice of the people,

Julius Caesar, Act 3, Scene 2

The final unintended consequence for the plotters is their destruction by the combined forces of Ocatvius, Antony, and their ally Lepidus. Along the way Caesar's political heirs have conducted a bloody purge of their opponents. In one scene we overhear Antony and his allies compiling the list of those to be killed, including their own relatives:

[Antony, Octavius, and Lepidus, seated at a table]

Antony
    These many, then, shall die; their names are prick'd [written].

Octavius
    Your brother too must die; consent you, Lepidus?

Lepidus
    I do consent—

Octavius
    Prick him down, Antony.

Lepidus
    Upon condition Publius shall not live,
    Who is your sister's son, Mark Antony.

Antony
He shall not live; look, with a spot I damn him.

Julius Caesar, Act 4, Scene 1

Here Shakespeare suggests the spreading circle of violence attendant to civil strife.

Julius Caesar is the very model of a coup. Shakespeare illuminates many of the essential elements of a plot to overthrow a ruler, and in particular he focuses on the central element, the behavior of the people involved. In this play Shakespeare creates many powerfully affecting images of humans caught up in extreme political violence, from the internal struggles in the minds of the conspirators to the fickleness of the citizenry, "blown like a feather" by the compelling and competing rhetoric of Brutus and Antony. Through the play we see the mix of personalities and motives of both the conspirators and their opponents, and their swiftly changing fortunes. Shakespeare draws out the key processes and dynamics as if using a hi-liter on history. He suggests that there is little to choose between Brutus and Antony and foreshadows the coming splintering of the Antony-Octavius-Lepidus triumvirate. But most importantly, he signals that it is individual people and what they do that count. What Shakespeare has done in *Julius Caesar* is to provide a case study in the complexity of human behavior in a coup. This kind of complexity challenges analysts; especially analysts dealing with only limited information as a coup is prepared or unfolds in a rush of events.

FAMILY MATTERS: HENRY VI AND RICHARD III

In your bride you bury brotherhood.

3 Henry VI, Act 4, Scene 1

Leadership and political analysts often must deal with the behavior of members of small groups or "inner circles," either as central political figures in their own right, or as close advisors to a principal leader. Family members, even extended family members, will often be part of or associated with these groups. Wives, brothers, sons and daughters, uncles, aunts, cousins can be found in, or on the edges, of many inner circles, and determining their roles and relative influence can be difficult. Shakespeare, coming from a society in which family mattered greatly, was sensitive to its role in politics and his plays raise important questions: Is "family" important in the politics of "tribal" or "lineal" societies? How do the relatives of leaders affect the political situation? Are family and political power inseparable in dynastic or traditional societies? What are the consequences of poor family political management?

The England Shakespeare dealt with in the history plays was dominated politically by large families. To a considerable degree family politics was the politics of the land. The Stanley, Percy, and Neville families, to name a few, were extended, lineal rather than nuclear, and were principal political factions. They controlled key positions in the government and church, wealth in the form of land, military force, and marriageable sons and daughters. These families were not merely social constructs; they were actors on the political, military, and economic landscapes, and dynasties unto themselves.

One such family was the Woodville's, whose ambitions lie behind much of the action in *Richard III*. In *3 Henry VI* we first encounter this family as a factor through the secret marriage of Elizabeth Woodville to Edward IV, the Yorkist successor to Henry VI. Elizabeth, a young widow and one of the great beauties of the age, was pursued and won by Edward after some struggle. With her came three problems. Her marriage to Edward was the cause of a personal rift with Warwick, and the related collapse of a potential alliance with France. She was a member of a numerous and ambitious family for which position, property, and spouses had to be found. And most importantly she produced a major change in the succession picture.

We first see Elizabeth as Lady Grey; the widow of Sir Richard Grey, who was killed fighting for the Yorkist cause. She is appealing to Edward, attempting to regain her husband's property seized by the Lancastrians. Edward, a great womanizer, is smitten. In order to have her he must marry her. This seemingly frivolous action causes Warwick to go over to the Lancastrian side, sets the increasingly ambitious Richard, Duke of Gloucester to plotting, and opens the door to her family's close access to the king and his patronage. From the start Edward's failure to manage his relationship with Elizabeth and her family creates fateful consequences.

The first of these is the break with Warwick. The acknowledged "kingmaker," Warwick is on a mission to France to secure Edward's political marriage to the sister of the French king. Learning of Edward's secret marriage, Warwick explodes:

Warwick
    King Lewis, I here protest, in sight of heaven,
    And by the hope I have of heavenly bliss,
    That I am clear from this misdeed of Edward's,
    No more my king, for he dishonours me,
    But most himself, if he could see his shame.

        3 Henry VI, Act 3, Scene 3

The immediate result is Warwick's defection to the cause of Henry VI and Margaret. The long-term effect is to significantly prolong and intensify the struggle between York and Lancaster.

The second outcome of the marriage is the creation of great tension between the faction represented by Queen Elizabeth and her family and a coalition of powerful magnates jealous of the rising power of the Woodvilles. In Act 4, Scene 1 of *3 Henry VI*, Shakespeare depicts the developing animosity caused by Edward's provision to his wife's family of significant marriages, and the titles and property that go with them. Beautiful, intelligent, and ambitious, Elizabeth has sought these favors for her family, and her success has bred powerful enemies. Responding to criticism that he has favored a Woodville over one of the most loyal of the Yorkist supporters, William Lord Hastings, Edward replies:

King Edward IV

 Ay, what of that? it was my will and grant;

 And for this once my will shall stand for law.

   3 Henry VI, Act 4, Scene 1

Edward's brother Richard, Duke of Gloucester, responds:

Gloucester

 And yet methinks your grace hath not done well,

 To give the heir and daughter of Lord Scales

 Unto the brother of your loving bride;

 She better would have fitted me or Clarence:

 But in your bride you bury brotherhood.

   3 Henry VI, Act 4, Scene 1

And brother Clarence adds:

Clarence

 Or else you would not have bestow'd the heir

 Of the Lord Bonville on your new wife's son,

 And leave your brothers to go speed elsewhere.

   3 Henry VI, Act 4, Scene 1

The rise of the Woodvilles creates rivalries within the family and between the King and other powerful lords that Richard will be able to exploit. These are realized in *Richard III*.

The third major consequence of the marriage is to extend Richard's particularly nasty path to the throne. The bachelor King Edward had no legitimate heirs, leaving open the possibility that one of his two brothers, Clarence or Richard, could succeed him. Any male offspring of Edward and Elizabeth would have primacy in succession. Richard had hoped that Edward would remain without legitimate heirs:

[Richard]

 Ay, Edward will use women honourably.

 Would he were wasted, marrow, bones and all,

 That from his loins no hopeful branch may spring,

 To cross me from the golden time I look for!

   3 Henry VI, Act 3, Scene 2

Richard must now count not only his brother Clarence as a potential successor ahead of his own claim, but also any sons born to Edward and Elizabeth. This will lead in *Richard III* to the coup against Edward's son and legitimate heir.

What Edward has done through his marriage is to create powerful animosities with his brothers. One, Clarence, defects to the Lancastrian side. The other, Richard, plots his violent course to the throne. Reacting to Clarence's defection, Richard reflects on his position:

Gloucester [Aside]
Not I:
My thoughts aim at a further matter; I
Stay not for the love of Edward, but the crown.

3 Henry VI, Act 4, Scene 1

In the first act of *Richard III,* Richard's plots are already well advanced, and he is exploiting the animosity building around the Queen as a means of stirring trouble for Edward:

Gloucester
Why, this it is, when men are ruled by women:
'Tis not the king that sends you to the Tower:
My Lady Grey his wife, Clarence, 'tis she
That tempers him to this extremity.
Was it not she and that good man of worship,
Anthony Woodville, her brother there,
That made him send Lord Hastings to the Tower,
From whence this present day he is deliver'd?
We are not safe, Clarence; we are not safe.

Richard III, Act 1, Scene 1

Hastings, newly "delivered" from the Tower, pledges to repay the Woodvilles for his imprisonment:

Hastings
But I shall live, my lord, to give them thanks
That were the cause of my imprisonment.

Richard III, Act 1, Scene 1

Richard will use Hastings as a pawn in his plot to seize the throne and destroy the Woodville family.

The Woodville's, however, do not represent an easy target. The Queen's brothers and sons are powerful lords and churchmen in their own right and resist Richard. The considerable Woodville family forces him to extend his campaign to such lengths that he begins to generate opposition even from his loyalists. Buckingham, his most important co-conspirator until Richard is crowned, equivocates when asked to murder Edward's young sons and heirs and eventually moves to armed opposition.

Elizabeth Woodville emerges as the strongest and most powerful member of the family. Her drive to protect Edward's male heir against Richard is doomed; but in the end she is successful in that her daughter will marry the future Henry VII. While Edward is unable to manage the family of his Queen, Richard is ultimately unable to defeat it.

Shakespeare reveals how families become important political factors in their own right, especially in lineal or dynastic societies. The broad social organizations that families represent provide networks of political, economic, military and personal influence, which can operate discreetly or openly to influence events. Understanding them is important, and penetrating them with traditional intelligence sources and methods can be challenging.

WHAT ABOUT THE WOMEN? MARGARET OF ANJOU IN HENRY VI

Away with her; go, bear her hence perforce.

3 Henry VI, Act 5, Scene 5

No leadership analyst can afford to ignore the role women play in politics, even in traditional, so-called male-dominated, societies. Mothers, wives, sisters, daughters and lovers, can exercise profound influence over men and events, even where they do not hold formal positions of power. For analysts there are many important questions about women: Can women play important political roles in traditional societies? What are these roles and what are their limits? What tools and methods do women have available? How do they actually exert power and influence? Under what circumstances can they emerge as political players in their own right? Do women have any special advantages? Shakespeare explored these questions in a society where few women held formal power, although one had enormous power.

Shakespeare's plays frequently depict women with important political roles. He recognized the often-decisive influence they exerted over male characters, as wives of powerful or ambitious men, as mothers seeking improved positions for their children, as lovers seeking security, and as powers in their own right. This power can be expressed as an intimate form of political behavior, the politics of the dinner table and the bedroom. But, sometimes, the role of the woman can become dominant and public.

Without doubt one of the strongest female characters in Shakespeare is Margaret of Anjou, Henry VI's wife and queen, but also his spine and brain. She is in many ways a female version of Richard III. Over the course of the three parts of *Henry VI* she becomes the leader of the Lancastrian party, its strategist, its driving force. She employs every weapon at her disposal—intellect, position, and sex—to achieve her goals. She plots the destruction of her rivals; and, although she does not fight in the physical sense, she is present at the important battles and shares in the risks and rewards. In cold blood she humiliates and kills her rival York. When her husband Henry physically and mentally collapses, she virtually divorces him and assumes leadership of her son's cause and the Lancastrian forces.

From the beginning Shakespeare shows that Margaret is politically astute and ambitious. In *1 Henry VI* we watch as she manipulates Suffolk's passion for her to achieve a political alliance between England and Anjou, an alliance beyond any reasonable expectation, and in the face of the strong opposition of some elements of the English nobility.

In *1 Henry VI* we first see Margaret as Suffolk's prisoner as a result of the war in France. Because of the relative poverty of her father's Kingdom of Anjou she is only a minor player in the political situation. But she reads Suffolk precisely. While personally drawn to him, she sees and grasps the political opportunity he presents. Suffolk's infatuation with her quickly leads to his successful attempt to arrange a marriage to Henry VI. In a society in which the marriages of the powerful were almost always political rather than romantic acts, this marriage gives Margaret the chance to be a great political player, and she takes it.

In *2 Henry VI* Margaret emerges as a power. In Act 1, Scene 3 she shows she has drawn the measure of the king. Addressing Suffolk, she says:

> His champions are the prophets and apostles,
> His weapons holy saws of sacred writ,
> His study is his tilt-yard, and his loves
> Are brazen images of canonized saints.
>
> *2 Henry VI,* Act 1, Scene 3

She has already indicated to Suffolk that she sees this situation is to her personal disadvantage:

Queen Margaret
> What shall King Henry be a pupil still
> Under the surly Gloucester's governance?
> Am I a queen in title and in style,
> And must be made a subject to a duke?
>
> *2 Henry VI,* Act 1, Scene 3

Margaret wants more than just the trappings of power, like Richard III she wants to exercise it. She is now fully engaged in the internal political contest and its bitter personal rivalries, with Suffolk as her chosen weapon:

Suffolk
> Madam, be patient: as I was cause
> Your highness came to England, so will I
> In England work your grace's full content
>
> *2 Henry VI,* Act 1, Scene 3

The first target of this weapon is Eleanor, wife of the Duke of Gloucester. In a plot that is both personal and political, Margaret and Suffolk use Eleanor's ambition to destroy her and weaken her husband.

As the king declines, Margaret becomes more powerful. By Act 4, Scene 9, Henry is lamenting the fates that made him king:

King Henry VI

> Was ever king that joy'd an earthly throne,
> And could command no more content than I?
> No sooner was I crept out of my cradle
> But I was made a king, at nine months old.
> Was never subject long'd to be a king
> As I do long and wish to be a subject.

2 Henry VI, Act 4, Scene 9

Margaret, however, is emerging as a commanding figure. Her liaisons with first Suffolk and, after his death, with Somerset, provide her powerful male allies. In the face of military defeat by the Yorkists at the Battle of Saint Albans, she presses the mentally paralyzed Henry to flee the field to preserve their cause for another day:

Queen Margaret

> If you be ta'en, we then should see the bottom
> Of all our fortunes: but if we haply scape,
> As well we may, if not through your neglect,
> We shall to London get, where you are loved
> And where this breach now in our fortunes made
> May readily be stopp'd.

2 Henry VI, Act 5, Scene 2

Here Margaret demonstrates both her power of decision and her political sophistication. She is the rising leader of the Lancastrian forces.

Margaret increasingly turns on her husband, investing all of her energy in insuring her son's future. After learning Henry has agreed that York will succeed him instead of his own son, Margaret declares to Henry her intention to carry on, even lead, the struggle:

> The northern lords that have forsworn thy colours
> Will follow mine, if once they see them spread;
> And spread they shall be, to thy foul disgrace
> And utter ruin of the house of York.
> Thus do I leave thee. Come, son, let's away;
> Our army is ready; come, we'll after them.

3 Henry VI, Act 1, Scene 1

Margaret loses the struggle with the Yorkists in the end, but not before she has exhausted all possible means, including alliances with Warwick, one of York's key allies, and with France. Even the deaths of her husband and son do not deter her. She is indeed much like *Richard III.* Margaret stands as a model of a talented and ambitious woman, able to exercise great power and influence, even in a traditional society where the political and military roles of women were sharply circumscribed by custom and law.

"MY LOYALTY IS SOMETIMES MY HONOR": LOYALTY AND HONOR IN KING JOHN

But for a kingdom any oath may be broken:
I would break a thousand oaths to reign one year.

3 Henry VI, Act 1, Scene 2

Loyalty and honor are critical to the operation of any organization or enterprise. No one, even the most powerful rulers in single party states, can rule alone. They depend on others at least for information and the carrying out of orders; and they depend on others to live up to their commitments, to act honorably. When neither loyalty nor honor can be counted on, rule becomes difficult and affairs of state chaotic.

Fluctuations in loyalty and honor are important elements in many political and military situations. The ability of intelligence analysts to accurately read both the loyalty of leaders and other principal actors and their strength of commitment can be vital in estimating the course of political and military situations. Analytical questions focusing on loyalty and honor include: Are loyalty and honor absolute or contingent? What is the basis for loyalty to political leaders? How is loyalty won and kept? What are the boundaries of loyalty? Is anyone totally loyal or completely honorable? Why do people break oaths or change sides in a political contest? What justifications do they employ? What are the political and military consequences of dishonorable actions?

Shakespeare explored the concept of loyalty, and the larger concept of honor, extensively in his histories and tragedies, not least of all because these were central concepts in the politics of his time. The 16th Century Catholic-Protestant divide alone furnished ample reason for divided loyalty. Throughout his plays, Shakespeare presents loyalty as a multifaceted phenomenon. He provides examples of individuals from those loyal unto death—Desdemona in Othello—to the most treacherous—Cassius in *Julius Caesar* and Iago in *Othello.* However, loyalty is not just for heroes. Even villains, some of King Richard's henchmen in *Richard III* for example, remain loyal to the end. He also shows us people who find issues of loyalty ambiguous or troubling, difficult to resolve, and who face critical decisions on where their loyalty lies. Shakespeare's implicit argument is that loyalty and honor are often both complex and contingent, as opposed to the then prevailing cultural "myth" that they were absolute.

King John, set in medieval England where honor was literally worn on the sleeves of the powerful, and oath taking was taken seriously, illustrates the conditionality of loyalty in the face of a complex reality. Few of the powerful in *King John* live up to either their word or established norms. Personal loyalty and honor are shredded by a host of factors including self-aggrandizement, appeals to higher goals, and tactical necessity. *King John* must have made the powerful around Elizabeth and James I more than a little nervous.

Loyalty in *King John* is strained by multiple elements in the personal and political situations of the key actors. There is an unresolved succession issue. John violates social norms when he seemingly has his nephew and potential competitor for the throne killed.

He engages in a fierce struggle with the church, forcing the powerful of the land to choose between king and God. The political and military fortunes of John and his opponents' rise and fall, offering the opportunity to switch sides for presumed advantage. John's capacity for rule fluctuates, causing others to weigh their political options. Both personal issues and political developments test family bonds. Thirteenth-century England was passing through a period of political turbulence, and loyalty and honor were early, if not the first, casualties.

In the opening scene, the first issue presented is the unresolved succession crisis precipitated by the death of King Richard the Lionhearted.[49] The contest had been temporarily resolved in John's favor; but powerful forces are gathering in support of John's nephew Arthur. John knows that until he can resolve the succession question he will always face divided loyalty and sit on an insecure throne. Receiving an ambassador from the King of France, John hears where France stands:

Chatillon
    Philip of France, in right and true behalf
    Of --
    Arthur Plantagenet, lays most lawful claim
    To this fair island and the territories,
    To Ireland, Poictiers, Anjou, Touraine, Maine,
    Desiring thee to lay aside the sword
    Which sways usurpingly these several titles,
    And put these same into young Arthur's hand,
    Thy nephew and right royal sovereign.

King John, Act 1, Scene 1

Here Shakespeare illustrates the dangers posed by a potential rival for the throne, one to whom the loyalties of others may become attached. In this case it is the French that are trying to exploit the situation by allying themselves with Arthur.

In the first act, Shakespeare introduces another of the elements challenging absolute loyalty in *King John,* the developing split between king and the Catholic Church. Speaking of his coming expedition against France the king states:

King John
    Our abbeys and our priories shall pay
    This expedition's charge.

King John, Act 1, Scene 1

John sees the church in England as an asset to be used for the purposes of the state. The church in Rome sees the state and the church in England as subordinate to its will in certain matters, including some worldly ones.

---

[49] Spiekerman, *Shakespeare's Political Realism,* 40.

Both John and the church resort to the most extreme measures to achieve their goals. John seizes church property, appoints church officials subservient to him, and refuses church direction. Rome excommunicates him, places all England under *interdict* (forbidding the practice of the sacraments), and aligns itself with John's foreign and domestic enemies. In a time when the moral and political power of the church was considerable, this conflict places loyalties to the king under extreme pressure. In response, some lords and commoners change sides.

Shakespeare uses the dramatic device of the fate of Arthur to suggest the weakening of personal bonds to the king. Initially John's nobles are loyal, recognizing that their interests are tied to his: "our weal, on you depending." Over time however, they become concerned that his obsessive need to secure the throne threatens all their interests, and directly threatens Arthur. Arthur's death while in John's custody leads some of the king's key followers to break with him. Announcing Arthur's demise, John is met with disdain on the part of the powerful lords Salisbury and Pembroke:

Salisbury
> It is apparent foul play; and 'tis shame
> That greatness should so grossly offer it:
> So thrive it in your game! and so, farewell.

Pembroke
> Stay yet, Lord Salisbury; I'll go with thee,
> And find the inheritance of this poor child,
> His little kingdom of a forced grave.
> That blood which owed the breadth of all this isle,
> Three foot of it doth hold: bad world the while!
> This must not be thus borne: this will break out
> To all our sorrows, and ere long I doubt.

> *King John,* Act 4, Scene 2

While the Lords Pembroke and Salisbury react emotionally to the murder of the child Arthur, they also calculate that John's action will lead to unrest and conflict at home, threatening their interests.

The citizens of the town of Angiers show the shrewd nature of the commoners. Besieged by both the English and the French, fighting in support of Arthur's claim to the throne, they ask the two "kings" to do battle to prove which is most deserving of their loyalty:

King John
> Acknowledge then the king, and let me in.

First Citizen
> That can we not; but he that proves the king,
> To him will we prove loyal: till that time
> Have we ramm'd up our gates against the world.

> *King John,* Act 2, Scene 1

When this fails they attempt to broker a political marriage arrangement between the two kingdoms to head off the sack of their town. There is no loyalty to king here, only self-interest.

The marriage arrangement is in fact a win-win situation for all, except for Arthur and the concept of honor. The French abandon Arthur and his cause for purposes of state. Meanwhile John, to remove Arthur as a problem, agrees to give up to the French a substantial portion of his kingdom. Shakespeare leaves it to one Philip Faulconbridge to give the lesson:

> Mad world! mad kings! mad composition [agreement]!
> John, to stop Arthur's title in the whole,
> Hath willingly departed with a part,
> And France, whose armour conscience buckled on,
> Whom zeal and charity brought to the field
> As God's own soldier, rounded in the ear
> With that same purpose-changer, that sly devil,
> That broker, that still breaks the pate of faith,
> That daily break-vow, he that wins of all,
> Of kings, of beggars, old men, young men, maids,
> Who, having no external thing to lose
> But the word 'maid,' cheats the poor maid of that,
> That smooth-faced gentleman, tickling Commodity [self-interest],
>
> *King John,* Act 2, Scene 1

The church itself is not above the exercise of statecraft. The pope and his agents wield both spiritual and temporal weapons against John for a time. On the brink of defeat at the hands of the French, the church, and his disaffected lords, John makes his peace with the pope and the pope turns on his French allies. Shakespeare makes it clear that what has changed is John's need for allies, not John himself:

Scene I King John's palace.

Enter King John, Cardinal Pandulph, and Attendants]

King John
    Thus have I yielded up into your hand
    The circle of my glory.

[Giving the crown]

Cardinal Pandulph
    Take again
    From this my hand, as holding of the pope
    Your sovereign greatness and authority.

King John

Now keep your holy word: go meet the French,
And from his holiness use all your power
To stop their marches 'fore we are inflamed.
Our discontented counties do revolt;
Our people quarrel with obedience,

King John, Act 5, Scene 1

And for its part the Church has made its own calculation:

Cardinal Pandulph
It was my breath that blew this tempest up,
Upon your stubborn usage of the pope...

Upon your oath of service to the pope,
Go I to make the French lay down their arms.

King John, Act 5, Scene 1

One can only doubt that these oaths will stand any more firmly than the others.

Nor are the French free from "situational honor." In an attempt to seize the throne of England, and in defiance of Cardinal Pandulph and the Church, the French Dauphin plots to murder his English allies once they have served their purpose, only to be preemptively betrayed by one of his own "honorable" nobles.

In *King John,* as well as in other plays, Shakespeare suggests that the political landscape of loyalty and honor is a rough one. While established social and cultural norms and personal commitments are elements of that landscape, shifting circumstances, evolving personal objectives, and dynamic social relationships also shape it. The challenge for analysts is to determine where individuals are located on that landscape, and how and in which directions they are moving over it. And most of the time analysts will be doing this with both incomplete information and limited understanding of the situation.

CONCLUSION

Shakespeare was writing political psychology before the term was invented, and the wealth of political and human factors explored in his work is vast. The subjects and material covered above represent only a fraction of what is in the Shakespeare canon.

Shakespeare's histories and tragedies cover a wide range of political activity and human behavior, from the most deeply personal—the crystallization in Richard II's mind of the world he has lost—to the most intensely political—Brutus' coup against Caesar and the civil war that follows. Perhaps most importantly, Shakespeare gives us a window into the cognitive and emotive elements of politics, what Harold Bloom has called "Shakespeare's uncanny power in the rendering of personality."[50] This window allows us, as analysts, to both observe how people think and act in vital situations, and ultimately to be more self-conscious about what we ourselves think about what we are observing.

Not least, Shakespeare allows us to recognize the incredible richness of the inner mental and behavioral worlds of leaders, worlds we can see only indistinctly, if at all, through our traditional collection means. Shakespeare provides us with images, metaphors, and models we can use to help shape and enrich our consideration of the issues and people we are concerned with today. He cannot tell us what Saddam Hussein is thinking at the moment, but he can help us to make out what it is like to think in ways and along paths similar to those of a Saddam Hussein. In re-creating the inner world of the minds of past leaders, he can assist us to peer inside the mind of our current "targets" and ourselves.

Political, strategic, or leadership analysts are asked to provide insight into issues and people who are remote: remote in time, perhaps; probably remote geographically and culturally; and definitely remote in experience. Shakespeare reveals to us a far distant culture, one with different beliefs about religion, family, women, loyalty and honor. A culture where "it" is about men not laws. Where the norms governing behavior are often quite different from our own. We ask our analysts today to enter into equally foreign cultures and divine the behavior of key political and military figures. What analyst today can claim to have managed an extended family or tribe, led a nation into war, built and broken alliances, faced defeat as the leader of a losing army, plotted a coup, justified a civil war, been betrayed by his closest associates, or murdered his way to a throne? Perhaps some have, at least in a figurative way, but for most these are beyond their professional experience. So how may we enhance our understanding of what it is like to be in such situations, to place our selves in like positions, to achieve empathy with our targets of interest, to "see" the current of cognition and sense the emotions involved in fateful events? Shakespeare provides a "distant mirror" by which to illuminate this remoteness. Analysts should read widely in Shakespeare to enlarge their sense for political behavior, to include enhancing their library of leadership images, metaphors and models. Analysts can also read directly in Shakespeare to examine particular issues, as was done in this paper. *Richard III* has something to say about Saddam Hussein, and *King John* something about the loyalty of Saddam's lieutenants.

Implicit in Shakespeare, however, is the understanding that we can probably never fully understand our targets of interest. This is an important lesson for political and leadership analysts and the consumers of their products. As Alexander Leggatt argues: "while a character's end may be known, his full nature is sometimes hidden from us, as though involvement in public life, demanding as it does the manipulation of appearances, leaves the character's inner self somewhat concealed from us, and perhaps even from him."[51] This is a useful caution against hard and fast intelligence judgments about foreign leaders.

Shakespeare does something else in the telling of his tales. He brought "storytelling" and "sense making" to a fine art. He was able to convey on multiple levels highly complex

---

[50] Bloom, *Shakespeare,* 6.
[51] Leggatt, *Shakespeare's Political Drama,* 242.

situations and personalities; multiple levels in the sense of both his effects on the audience and the fullness of the subject matter. He appealed to both the reason and the emotion of his audience, and his characters and contexts are vivid and compelling.

Finally, Shakespeare provides lessons in the power of quality writing. In the words of Russ McDonald:

The skill at encoding information—and encoding so much information—in the mesmerizing verbal medium is one of the gifts that made Shakespeare a greater dramatist than any of his contemporaries... [52]

As we go down the road to "digital production" and "knowledge packets," concepts that are fundamentally antithetical to story telling and sense making, it will be increasingly important that quality writing continue to be one of the essential elements by which we measure quality analysis.

As his skills as a playwright matured, Shakespeare hardly wasted a word. Thousands of words have been written about Saddam Hussein, but none convey the character of such a person as well as these few lines spoken by Shakespeare's Richard III:

...I am in
So far in blood that sin will pluck on sin:
Tear-falling pity dwells not in this eye.

Richard III, Act 4, Scene 2

---

[52] McDonald, *Shakespeare and the Arts of Language,* 8.

SOURCES CONSULTED

In addition to *Arden, Cambridge, Signet, Folger* and Internet versions of the texts of the plays, the author has consulted the following:

Bate, Jonathan. *The Genius of Shakespeare.* London: Picador, 1998.

Bevington, David. *Shakespeare.* Oxford: Blackwell Publishing, 2002.

Bloom, Harold. *Shakespeare: The Invention of the Human.* New York: Riverhead Books, 1998.

_____. *The Western Canon: the Books and School of the Ages.* New York: Riverhead Books, 1994.

Boyce, Charles. *Shakespeare: The Essential Reference to His Plays, His Poems, His Life, and More.* New York: Dell Publishing, 1990.

Bozeman, Adda B. *Politics and Culture in International History: From the Ancient Near East to the Opening of the Modern Age.* 2d edition. New Brunswick: Transaction Publishers, 2002.

Brown, John Russell. *Shakespeare and the Theatrical Event.* New York: Palgrave Mac-Millan, 2002.

Crane, Milton. "Introduction to Henry VI Part Three," *The Signet Classic Shakespeare. New York:* Penguin, 1968.

Darragi, Rafiq. "Arab World," in *The Oxford Companion to Shakespeare.* Michael Dobson and Stanley Wells, eds. Oxford: Oxford University Press, 2001.

Dockray, Keith. *William Shakespeare, the Wars of the Roses, and the Historians.* Charleston, S.C.: Tempus Publishing Inc., 2002.

Du Boulay, F.R.H. *An Age of Ambition: English Society in the Late Middle Ages.* New York: The Viking Press, 1970.

Gillingham, John. *The Wars of the Roses: Peace and Conflict in Fifteenth Century England.* London: Phoenix Press, 2001.

Hattaway, Michael. "Introduction," in *The First Part of King Henry VI,* The New Cambridge Shakespeare, Michael Hattaway, ed. Cambridge: Cambridge University Press, 1990.

He, Quixin. "China," in *The Oxford Companion to Shakespeare.* Michael Dobson and Stanley Wells, eds. Oxford: Oxford University Press, 2001.

Leggatt, Alexander. *Shakespeare's Political Drama: the History Plays and the Roman Plays.* New York: Routledge, 1988.

Loomba, Ania. "India", in *The Oxford Companion to Shakespeare.* Michael Dobson and Stanley Wells, Stanley, eds. Oxford: Oxford University Press, 2001.

Machiavelli, Niccolo. *The Prince,* 2d ed., Robert M. Adams, trans. New York: W.W. Norton & Company, 1992.

McDonald, Russ. *Shakespeare and the Arts of Language.* Oxford: Oxford University Press, 2001.

Norwich, John Julius. *Shakespeare's Kings: The Great Plays and the History of England in the Middle Ages.* New York: Simon and Schuster, 1999.

Renaissance Films, "Henry V," 1989.

Rosenbaum, Ron. *Explaining Hitler: The Search for the Origins of His Evil.* New York: Random House, 1998.

Saccio, Peter. *Shakespeare's English Kings: History, Chronicle, and Drama.* Oxford: Oxford University Press, 2000.

Snow, C. P. *The Two Cultures.* Cambridge: Cambridge University Press, 1998.

Spiekerman, Tim. *Shakespeare's Political Realism: The English History Plays.* New York: State University of New York Press, 2001.

Tuchman, Barbara W. *A Distant Mirror: The Calamitous 14th Century.* New York; Ballantine Books, 1978.

United Artists, "Richard III," 1995.

ABOUT THE AUTHOR

In October 2002, Jeffrey B. White completed a thirty-four year career with the Defense Intelligence Agency, having served in a wide variety of senior analytical and leadership positions. Among the positions he held were: imagery analyst, military capabilities analyst, current intelligence analyst, senior analyst for the Arab-Israeli confrontation states, Chief of the Middle East current intelligence division, Chief of the Office for Middle East/Africa Military Assessments, and Chief, Regional Military Assessments. Mr. White is now an associate with the Washington Institute for Near East Policy and an independent consultant.

While with DIA, Mr. White was involved as an intelligence officer in every Middle East crisis from the 1968 Arab-Israeli War of Attrition to the developing conflict with Iraq in 2002. He led numerous crisis intelligence response groups within the agency, including those dealing with the Lebanese civil war, Israeli-Syrian conflict in Lebanon, U.S. operations against Libya, U.S. naval operations in the Persian Gulf, multiple Iraqi crises from 1994 to 2000, and the conflict with Afghanistan.

Mr. White holds a BA in Foreign Affairs from the University of Virginia, and an MA in International Affairs from George Washington University, both with Near East specialties. He has received numerous awards for service as an intelligence officer, including the Secretary of Defense Medal for Meritorious Civilian Service, the National Intelligence Distinguished Service Medal, and the DIA Director's awards for both Exceptional and Meritorious Civilian Service.

Joint Military Intelligence College

Occasional Papers

Unclassified papers are available through <*www.ntis.gov*>; selected papers are available through the U.S. Government Printing Office <*www.gpo.gov*>.

1. Classified paper.

2. *Getting Intelligence Right: The Power of Logical Procedure,* Capt (USAF) William S. Brei, 1996.

3. *An Office Manager's Guide to Intelligence Readiness,* Russell G. Swenson, 1996.

4. Classified paper.

5. *A Flourishing Craft: Teaching Intelligence Studies,* Papers Prepared for the 18 June 1999 JMIC Conference on Teaching Intelligence Studies at Colleges and Universities, 1999.

6. *Intelligence Essentials for Everyone,* Lisa Krizan, 1999.

7. *Intelligence Analysis in Theater Joint Intelligence Centers: An Experiment in Applying Structured Methods,* MSgt (USAF), Robert D. Folker, Jr., 2000.

8. *Dangerous Assumption: Preparing the U.S. Intelligence Warning System for the New Millennium,* Jan Goldman, 2000.

9. *The Creation of the National Imagery and Mapping Agency: The Congressional Oversight Role,* Anne Daugherty Miles, 2001.

10. *Shakespeare for Analysts: Literature and Intelligence,* Jeffrey White, 2003.

www.ingramcontent.com/pod-product-compliance
Lightning Source LLC
Chambersburg PA
CBHW072111280526
45788CB00006B/2493